RICHARD WRIGHT

BIOGRAPHY

THE REMARKABLE STORY OF THE KEYBOARDIST WHO SHAPED PINK FLOYD AND REDEFINED MODERN ROCK

CURTIS A. NELSON

TABLE OF CONTENT

INTRODUCTION   **9**

CHAPTER 1   **17**

EARLY LIFE AND CHILDHOOD   **17**
EARLY EXPOSURE TO MUSIC, FIRST INSTRUMENTS, AND
CHILDHOOD INFLUENCES   19
SCHOOL LIFE, EARLY EDUCATION, AND BUDDING INTEREST
IN THE ARTS   21
KEY MOMENTS THAT SHAPED HIS PERSONALITY AND
MUSICAL CURIOSITY   23

CHAPTER 2   **25**

MEETING FUTURE BANDMATES   **25**
MEETING ROGER WATERS, NICK MASON, AND SYD
BARRETT   27
FORMATION OF THE EARLY BAND AND INITIAL
COLLABORATIONS   29
EARLY MUSICAL EXPERIMENTS AND PERFORMANCES   30

CHAPTER 3   **33**

THE BIRTH OF PINK FLOYD   **33**

EARLY GIGS, FIRST RECORDINGS, AND INITIAL AUDIENCE
RECEPTION   35
RICHARD'S ROLE AS KEYBOARDIST AND VOCALIST IN
SHAPING THE BAND'S SOUND   37
DEVELOPING THE DISTINCTIVE PINK FLOYD ATMOSPHERE
AND STYLE   38

CHAPTER 4   41

EARLY ALBUMS AND MUSICAL GROWTH   41
MUSICAL EXPERIMENTATION AND DEVELOPMENT OF THE
PSYCHEDELIC SOUND   43
SONGWRITING CONTRIBUTIONS AND SOLO PARTS WITHIN
EARLY TRACKS   44
RELATIONSHIP DYNAMICS WITHIN THE BAND DURING
EARLY YEARS   46

CHAPTER 5   49

BREAKTHROUGH WITH DARK SIDE OF THE MOON   49
RICHARD'S KEYBOARD WORK ON TRACKS LIKE THE GREAT
GIG IN THE SKY AND US AND THEM   51
CREATIVE PROCESS AND STUDIO INNOVATIONS   53
IMPACT OF THE ALBUM ON THE BAND'S CAREER AND ON
ROCK MUSIC GLOBALLY   54

CHAPTER 6   57

LIFE BEHIND THE SCENES   57

CONTRIBUTIONS TO THE BAND'S ARRANGEMENTS AND
TEXTURES   58
BALANCING PERSONAL LIFE WITH BAND COMMITMENTS 60
EARLY STRUGGLES WITH RECOGNITION AND CREATIVE
CONTROL   62

CHAPTER 7   **65**

WISH YOU WERE HERE AND ANIMALS   **65**
THE MAKING OF ANIMALS AND RICHARD'S ROLE IN
CONCEPTUAL TRACKS   67
COLLABORATION CHALLENGES AND INTERPERSONAL
TENSIONS WITHIN THE BAND   68
HIGHLIGHTS OF LIVE PERFORMANCES AND TOURS DURING
THIS ERA   70

CHAPTER 8   **72**

TENSIONS AND THE WALL   **72**
RICHARD'S DIMINISHING ROLE AND TEMPORARY
DEPARTURE   74
SESSION WORK AND TOURING CONTRIBUTIONS DESPITE
INTERNAL STRUGGLES   76
REFLECTIONS ON CREATIVE DIFFERENCES AND PERSONAL
GROWTH   78

CHAPTER 9   **80**

SOLO WORK AND PERSONAL PROJECTS   **80**

MUSICAL STYLE, THEMES, AND RECEPTION OF HIS SOLO
ALBUMS   82
COLLABORATIONS OUTSIDE OF PINK FLOYD   84
LESSONS LEARNED FROM WORKING INDEPENDENTLY   86

CHAPTER 10   **88**

RETURN TO PINK FLOYD   **88**
ROLE IN THE DIVISION BELL AND REUNION DYNAMICS   90
CONTRIBUTIONS TO LIVE TOURS AND RECORDINGS   91
REGAINING RECOGNITION AND RESPECT WITHIN THE BAND
                                                         93

CHAPTER 11   **96**

MUSICAL STYLE AND LEGACY   **96**
INFLUENCE ON PINK FLOYD'S OVERALL STYLE AND ROCK
MUSIC   98
ANALYSIS OF KEY SONGS AND ALBUMS   99
COMPARISON WITH CONTEMPORARIES AND INNOVATORS
OF THE TIME   101

CHAPTER 12   **104**

PERSONAL LIFE AND CHALLENGES   **104**
HEALTH STRUGGLES, EMOTIONAL CHALLENGES, AND
PERSONAL REFLECTIONS   106
HOW PERSONAL EXPERIENCES INFLUENCED HIS MUSIC 108

STORIES THAT REVEAL HIS CHARACTER AND RESILIENCE
109

CHAPTER 13   112

LATER YEARS AND LAST CONTRIBUTIONS   112
COLLABORATIONS, INTERVIEWS, AND PUBLIC
APPEARANCES   113
FINAL RECORDINGS AND PROJECTS   115
LEGACY-BUILDING ACTIONS BEFORE HIS PASSING   117

CHAPTER 14   120

DEATH AND POSTHUMOUS RECOGNITION   120
REACTIONS FROM FANS, PEERS, AND THE MUSIC INDUSTRY
121
AWARDS, TRIBUTES, AND MEMORIAL EVENTS   123
THE ENDURING IMPACT OF HIS LIFE AND MUSIC   125

CHAPTER 15   128

LEGACY AND INFLUENCE   128
INSPIRATION TO FUTURE GENERATIONS OF MUSICIANS 130
THE LASTING IMPORTANCE OF HIS WORK WITH PINK FLOYD
131
REFLECTIONS ON HIS LIFE, CAREER, AND ENDURING
PRESENCE IN MUSIC HISTORY   133

INTRODUCTION

Richard Wright remains one of the most influential yet often underappreciated figures in the history of modern rock music. As the keyboardist and a founding member of Pink Floyd, his contributions were integral to the band's distinctive sound, shaping their musical identity across decades of innovation, experimentation, and groundbreaking recordings. Wright's story is one of quiet brilliance, marked by an extraordinary capacity to blend technical mastery with emotional sensitivity, creating music that continues to resonate with fans around the world. From his early life in Hatch End, Middlesex, to his final contributions before his death in 2008, Wright's journey reflects a commitment to artistry, collaboration, and the subtle power of musical expression.

Born on July 28, 1943, Richard William Wright grew up in a period marked by social change, artistic exploration, and the post-war evolution of British music. His early life provided both inspiration and grounding, shaping the sensibilities that would later define his musical approach. The environments he inhabited, from his family home to his schools, offered him access to both formal education and informal artistic exposure. Wright displayed a natural aptitude for music from a young age, developing an affinity for piano and keyboards that would form the foundation of his professional career. This early passion for music was nurtured by his curiosity, discipline, and willingness to explore sound in creative ways. Wright's formative experiences instilled in him a sensitivity to melody, harmony, and texture that would become hallmarks of his style.

During his school years, Wright immersed himself in the study of music while also exploring other artistic disciplines. He demonstrated an early understanding of composition, arrangement, and improvisation, experimenting with different instruments and techniques. These formative experiences cultivated a deep appreciation for the role of keyboards in shaping the emotional and structural aspects of music. Wright's exposure to classical music, jazz, and contemporary popular music allowed him to synthesize diverse influences, developing a unique approach that balanced sophistication with accessibility. His early education also instilled a sense of curiosity and openness, qualities that would underpin his collaborative work with Pink Floyd and his ability to adapt to evolving musical landscapes.

Wright's journey to professional recognition began in earnest during his college years at Regent Street Polytechnic, where he studied architecture. While his academic focus was initially directed toward a different discipline, it was during this period that he met future Pink Floyd bandmates Roger Waters, Nick Mason, and Syd

Barrett. These encounters would prove transformative, setting the stage for the formation of one of the most innovative and enduring rock bands of the twentieth century. Wright's architectural studies, which emphasized structure, balance, and creativity, complemented his musical inclinations, reinforcing his appreciation for design, pattern, and harmony in sound. The intersection of these experiences would inform his approach to music, enabling him to construct sonic landscapes that were simultaneously intricate and cohesive.

The formation of Pink Floyd emerged from a combination of personal chemistry, shared artistic vision, and a mutual desire to explore new musical frontiers. As a keyboardist, Wright brought an essential voice to the ensemble, providing harmonic depth, melodic support, and textural richness. From the early days of performing at local venues to the development of the band's first recordings, his contributions were central to the evolution of Pink Floyd's sound. Wright's ability to craft immersive atmospheres, support complex arrangements, and enhance the emotional impact of songs distinguished him as a musician whose presence was both indispensable and transformative.

Throughout Pink Floyd's career, Wright demonstrated an exceptional capacity for innovation. His work on albums such as The Piper at the Gates of Dawn, A Saucerful of Secrets, Meddle, and Atom Heart Mother established him as a forward-thinking keyboardist capable of blending classical sensibilities with contemporary rock and experimental textures. He pioneered techniques that expanded the role of synthesizers and electric pianos in rock music, creating soundscapes that were both complex and emotionally resonant. Wright's sensitivity to dynamics, harmony, and spatial awareness allowed Pink Floyd to explore progressive and psychedelic directions, defining their unique aesthetic and influencing generations of musicians who would follow.

One of the defining moments of Wright's career came with the creation of The Dark Side of the Moon, an album that not only solidified Pink Floyd's global reputation but also showcased his unparalleled skills as a composer and keyboardist. Wright's work on tracks such as Us and Them, The Great Gig in the Sky, and Time exemplified his ability to integrate melodic phrasing, harmonic sophistication, and atmospheric textures. His contributions were subtle yet critical, demonstrating the power of restraint and sensitivity in music. By creating layers of sound that supported lyrical content and thematic exploration, Wright helped craft an album that remains a benchmark in rock history, demonstrating the potential of keyboards to shape the emotional and structural core of music.

Beyond his technical skills, Wright's artistry was defined by his collaborative spirit. He understood the importance of listening, responding, and enhancing the contributions of his bandmates. His musical intelligence allowed him to anticipate shifts in melody, rhythm, and mood, crafting arrangements that complemented the creative visions of the group while maintaining his own expressive voice. Wright's humility and willingness to prioritize the collective sound over personal spotlight reinforced the cohesion and distinctive character of Pink Floyd, illustrating the profound impact that subtlety, sensitivity, and collaboration can have on artistic success.

As Pink Floyd evolved, Wright faced both triumphs and challenges. Interpersonal tensions, shifting creative dynamics, and periods of estrangement tested his resilience, yet he continued to contribute meaningfully to the band's projects. His ability to navigate complex professional relationships, maintain artistic integrity, and sustain a high level of musical output speaks to his character and dedication. Wright's approach to challenges was defined by reflection, patience, and an unwavering focus on musical quality, allowing him to leave an enduring imprint on both individual albums and the collective trajectory of Pink Floyd.

In addition to his work with the band, Wright pursued solo projects and collaborations that reflected his personal artistic vision. Albums such as Wet Dream allowed him to explore musical ideas outside the constraints of the band's collective identity, further demonstrating his versatility and creativity. These projects offered insight into Wright's compositional preferences, melodic sensibilities, and textural experimentation, reinforcing his status as a multi-dimensional artist capable of balancing technical mastery with expressive depth. Through his solo work, Wright demonstrated that his musical genius extended beyond group performance, contributing to the broader landscape of contemporary rock and keyboard-driven music.

Wright's influence extended to live performances, where his artistry was showcased in both subtle embellishments and expansive sonic textures. Concerts were opportunities for him to translate studio techniques into dynamic stage experiences, creating immersive atmospheres that captivated audiences. His interplay with guitarists, vocalists, and percussionists demonstrated a keen understanding of ensemble dynamics, reinforcing the emotional and structural impact of Pink Floyd's music in real time. These performances highlighted his role not only as a keyboardist but as a pivotal architect of mood, tension, and release, shaping the audience's experience and deepening the impact of the music.

The legacy of Richard Wright is not limited to his technical innovations or compositional achievements. It also encompasses the influence he has had on generations of musicians who continue to draw inspiration from his work. Keyboardists, composers, and producers recognize Wright's approach to harmony, texture, and atmosphere as a model for balancing creativity with subtlety. His contributions exemplify the potential for keyboards to serve as both a structural foundation and an expressive voice, expanding the possibilities of rock music and progressive composition. Wright's artistry demonstrates that influence is often most profound when it is understated, collaborative, and emotionally intelligent.

In reflecting on Wright's life, it is clear that his story is as much about personal character as it is about musical accomplishment. He exemplified qualities of humility, perseverance, and artistic integrity, demonstrating that enduring success is built on dedication to craft, sensitivity to collaboration, and a commitment to excellence. His life provides lessons not only for musicians but for anyone seeking to understand the interplay between talent, discipline, and the subtle power of creative contribution. Wright's journey from a young music enthusiast in Middlesex to a global icon of rock music underscores the transformative potential of dedication, vision, and artistic courage.

Richard Wright's passing in 2008 marked the end of a remarkable chapter in music history, yet his influence endures. His compositions, performances, and innovations continue to resonate across generations, influencing contemporary rock, progressive music, ambient compositions, and the approach of keyboardists worldwide. The subtlety, sophistication, and emotional resonance that defined his work remain a touchstone for aspiring musicians and established artists alike, ensuring that his legacy remains vibrant, relevant, and celebrated.

This biography seeks to illuminate the life and career of Richard Wright in a comprehensive, detailed, and nuanced manner. It explores his formative years, his rise within Pink Floyd, his individual artistry, his contributions to landmark albums, and his influence on modern rock music. Through a careful examination of his recordings, performances, collaborations, and personal journey, this book aims to provide insight into both the man and the musician, capturing the essence of a creative spirit whose work shaped the trajectory of rock music and left an indelible mark on the cultural landscape.

By exploring Wright's life from multiple perspectives, including musical, personal, and historical, this biography demonstrates how a single musician's vision, talent, and dedication can redefine artistic possibilities. Wright's story is not only one of technical skill and compositional brilliance but also a testament to the power of subtlety, collaboration, and integrity. His contributions to Pink Floyd and modern rock stand as enduring proof that music, when approached with intelligence, sensitivity, and creativity, can resonate across time, generations, and cultures.

CHAPTER 1

Early Life and Childhood

Richard William Wright was born on July 28, 1943, in Hatch End, a suburban area within the borough of Harrow, in Middlesex, England. His arrival came during one of the most turbulent periods in modern history, as the Second World War was still raging across Europe. London and its surrounding areas were not immune from the bombings, and many families lived with the constant anxiety of air raids and wartime scarcity. Although he was too young to remember much of the war's direct impact, the environment of uncertainty, rationing, and community resilience formed the backdrop of his earliest years. These conditions were shared by his entire generation, shaping their outlook on life and contributing to the spirit of postwar creativity that would later permeate British music and culture.

Richard was the son of a prosperous family. His father, Cedric Wright, was a successful biochemist who worked in medical research, while his mother, Bridie, was a homemaker who placed great emphasis on stability and nurturing within the family. The Wright household in Hatch End was comfortable compared to many wartime families. This stability gave Richard the opportunity to grow up in an environment where education and culture were valued. Unlike many of his contemporaries who were raised in working-class conditions, Richard's middle-class upbringing exposed him early on to opportunities in the arts, particularly music.

Hatch End itself was a suburban community located northwest of central London, characterized by modest houses, gardens, and a quiet atmosphere. During Richard's childhood, the area was beginning to transform from its earlier semi-rural identity into a more suburban setting as families moved out of central London in search of safer and more spacious homes. The presence of greenery, parks, and relative tranquility offered Richard a childhood that combined suburban comfort with access to the cultural vibrancy of London, which was only a short train ride away. This duality of peaceful retreat and cultural exposure would prove important later, as Wright often sought solace in quiet, reflective environments while also thriving in the artistic hubbub of city life.

Within his family, Richard was known to be shy and introspective. Unlike children who sought constant attention, he had a quiet curiosity about the world. His parents encouraged him to pursue his interests, and while they were not artists themselves, they recognized his early fascination with sounds and melodies. This support, though not overtly forceful, gave him the freedom to explore his growing passion for music without the pressure of strict expectations. Wright would later recall that music seemed to come naturally to him rather than being imposed, and this gentle encouragement from his parents laid the foundation for his lifelong relationship with the art form.

Early Exposure to Music, First Instruments, and Childhood Influences

Richard's earliest connection with music came through the radio, which was an essential fixture in most British homes during the 1940s and 1950s. Families often gathered around to listen to news, variety programs, and musical broadcasts. The BBC's classical and light entertainment offerings were central to this experience, and it was through these broadcasts that Wright first became acquainted with music. He absorbed the sounds of orchestral works, light jazz, and popular postwar songs. These early impressions would stay with him, instilling a taste for melody, harmony, and atmosphere.

At a young age, Richard showed an instinctive ability to pick up tunes and experiment with them. His parents soon realized his natural aptitude and arranged for him to take piano lessons. The piano became his first true instrument, and it quickly turned into a central part of his life. Unlike some children who view lessons as a chore, Richard found fascination in the keys, chords, and progressions. The instrument provided him with a means of expression that suited his reflective and gentle personality. He would spend

19

long hours practicing, not out of obligation but because of the genuine joy he felt in exploring its possibilities.

Classical music formed the foundation of his early training. Composers such as Bach, Mozart, and Chopin introduced him to the concepts of harmony, counterpoint, and structure. But it was not only the strict classical discipline that appealed to him. He was also intrigued by the more atmospheric and emotive qualities of romantic and impressionist composers. Later in his youth, Richard found himself drawn to the works of Debussy and Ravel, whose lush harmonies and dreamlike textures deeply resonated with his sensibilities. This exposure would play a vital role in the development of his own style, which favored mood, color, and depth over technical showmanship.

Beyond classical traditions, the growing influence of jazz in postwar Britain made its way into Richard's ears. American jazz records were circulating, and figures such as Duke Ellington, Thelonious Monk, and Bill Evans introduced an entirely different world of rhythm and improvisation. Jazz appealed to Wright's sense of freedom, and he admired how musicians could weave spontaneous melodies over complex harmonies. His experimentation with jazz chords on the piano gradually expanded his musical vocabulary, giving him tools that would later define his contributions to Pink Floyd's sound.

Another influence during his childhood came from his environment itself. Growing up in a leafy suburb, Richard often found inspiration in nature, which fueled his preference for reflective and atmospheric sounds. This connection between environment and music would later reappear in Pink Floyd's work, where landscapes and atmospheres played crucial roles in the mood of their albums.

School Life, Early Education, and Budding Interest in the Arts

Richard attended the local schools in Hatch End, where he was regarded as a quiet but thoughtful student. Teachers often noticed his reserved demeanor, but also recognized his ability to focus deeply on subjects that captured his imagination. While not the most outspoken in class, he possessed an inner creativity that came alive whenever artistic subjects were introduced.

In addition to his academic studies, Richard participated in music-related activities at school. He often played piano at assemblies or contributed to school concerts, where his talent gradually became recognized by both peers and teachers. Although he was never a flamboyant performer, his sensitivity to tone and atmosphere distinguished him from other students. These performances boosted his confidence and made him realize that his talent could reach others, even if his personality remained modest and unassuming.

While music was clearly his strongest interest, Wright also developed a budding fascination with visual arts and design.

He enjoyed sketching and exploring artistic ideas, which revealed his broader creative mindset. This interest in the arts would eventually guide him toward studying architecture at Regent Street Polytechnic, where he met the future members of Pink Floyd. At this early stage, however, art functioned as a complementary passion that deepened his appreciation of creativity in multiple forms.

Despite his academic strengths, Richard's natural inclination was not toward rigid structure but toward expression and imagination. Subjects like mathematics or sciences did not hold his attention as much as those that allowed for interpretation and creativity. This sometimes caused friction with the formal demands of schoolwork, but his teachers generally encouraged his artistic leanings, recognizing his potential.

Outside of school, Richard spent much of his time practicing piano, listening to records, and attending concerts whenever possible. London offered numerous opportunities to experience live performances, and trips to the city exposed him to orchestras, jazz clubs, and other cultural events. These outings broadened his horizons and reinforced his growing conviction that music was more than a pastime. It was becoming central to his identity.

Key Moments That Shaped His Personality and Musical Curiosity

Several defining moments in Richard Wright's childhood helped shape both his personality and his lifelong relationship with music. One of the earliest was the discovery of how sound could evoke emotion. As a child, he was fascinated by the way a single chord could feel uplifting, melancholic, or mysterious. He often experimented at the piano, not only playing assigned pieces but also inventing small progressions of his own. This habit of exploration reflected his natural curiosity and set him apart from students who only approached music as an academic subject.

Another key moment came when he first encountered jazz in greater depth. Unlike classical works that followed predictable structures, jazz offered a sense of unpredictability and flow. The realization that music could be improvised, that it could exist in the moment without being written down, captivated him. This freedom aligned with his personality, which sought expression without confrontation. He preferred to let music speak for him rather than asserting himself through words or social dominance.

Richard's reserved character was also shaped by his family life. Growing up in a supportive but not overly demanding household gave him a sense of quiet confidence. He learned to value independence and self-reflection, traits that would later define his approach within a band setting. While other musicians might have sought the spotlight, Richard was content to remain in the background, contributing atmosphere, color, and depth to the collective sound. His personality and musical role would remain closely linked throughout his life.

A further defining influence came from the cultural shifts of postwar Britain. The late 1940s and 1950s were a time of reconstruction and renewal. Young people were beginning to develop a cultural identity distinct from their parents. The emergence of rock and roll in the 1950s provided Richard and his peers with an entirely new form of musical energy. Though his deepest influences lay in classical and jazz, the rise of rock music created the conditions for experimentation, blending traditions, and exploring new sonic landscapes. Wright, open-minded and curious, absorbed this atmosphere of innovation and carried it into his own work.

CHAPTER 2

Meeting Future Bandmates

After completing his early education, Richard Wright enrolled at Regent Street Polytechnic in London, where he pursued studies in architecture. The Polytechnic offered a rigorous and stimulating environment that combined technical training with artistic exploration. For Richard, the study of architecture was not just a vocational choice but also an extension of his creative interests. Architecture appealed to him because it demanded both precision and imagination, technical skill and aesthetic judgment. It allowed him to explore the balance between structure and creativity, a balance that would later be reflected in his approach to music composition and arrangement.

During his years at the Polytechnic, Richard was immersed in a vibrant community of students from diverse backgrounds. The atmosphere was intellectually stimulating, filled with debates, collaborative projects, and exposure to contemporary artistic movements. While architecture was the formal focus of his studies, Richard found himself increasingly drawn to the broader cultural environment, which included music, literature, and experimental art. His studies encouraged discipline, planning, and attention to detail, all qualities that he later applied to his meticulous approach to keyboard playing and studio work.

The Polytechnic years were also a time of personal growth and self-discovery. Richard, previously reserved and introspective, began to develop a sense of independence and confidence. He explored his tastes, experimented with new ideas, and encountered peers who shared his interests in creativity and innovation. These formative experiences helped him cultivate a mindset that valued both collaboration and individual expression. He was learning to navigate complex projects, manage time effectively, and think critically about form and function, all of which became essential skills when he transitioned into collaborative music-making with his future bandmates.

While the study of architecture was demanding, Richard never allowed it to overshadow his passion for music. He often spent evenings and weekends playing the piano, experimenting with chords, and exploring musical concepts. His ability to balance rigorous academic work with musical exploration demonstrated early on the discipline, focus, and commitment that would define his professional life. The Polytechnic provided both a foundation for practical skills and a backdrop for the formative encounters that would eventually lead to the creation of Pink Floyd.

Meeting Roger Waters, Nick Mason, and Syd Barrett

It was during his time at Regent Street Polytechnic that Richard Wright met fellow students who would become central figures in his life and career. Among them were Roger Waters, Nick Mason, and later Syd Barrett, whose arrival would complete the early lineup that transformed the London music scene. Each of these individuals brought a unique personality, skill set, and creative energy to the group, and Richard quickly recognized the potential for collaboration.

Roger Waters, who was also studying architecture, shared Richard's interest in artistic expression and conceptual thinking. Waters had a strong sense of ambition, a keen intellect, and a drive to explore the emotional and philosophical dimensions of music. Richard found in Waters a partner who complemented his own musical sensibilities, combining technical skill with imaginative ideas. Their friendship grew out of shared classes, studio projects, and conversations about art, design, and the cultural currents of the time.

Nick Mason, another fellow student, had a deep passion for rhythm, sound, and the mechanics of musical performance. Mason's approach was both precise and inventive, emphasizing the importance of timing, experimentation, and texture. Richard recognized Mason's abilities as both a collaborator and a stabilizing presence in the group. The three began to explore musical ideas together, often meeting outside the classroom to discuss, practice, and experiment.

Syd Barrett, who had a more eccentric and unpredictable personality, brought an entirely different energy to the group. His creativity was raw, uninhibited, and infused with a sense of whimsy and surrealism. Although Richard and Barrett initially had contrasting temperaments, the combination of Barrett's visionary ideas with Richard's musical skill created a powerful synergy. Barrett's arrival marked a turning point in their musical journey, as he introduced experimental techniques, unusual song structures, and a distinctive lyrical style that challenged and inspired the others.

The meeting of these four individuals was not a simple coincidence. The cultural environment of London in the early 1960s, combined with the Polytechnic's emphasis on creativity and experimentation, created fertile ground for collaboration. Their interactions were marked by curiosity, mutual respect, and a shared desire to explore new musical possibilities. Richard quickly became aware that these relationships could evolve into something significant, laying the foundation for the early formation of what would become Pink Floyd.

Formation of the Early Band and Initial Collaborations

The early collaborations between Richard Wright, Roger Waters, Nick Mason, and Syd Barrett were informal at first but quickly became more structured as their shared vision for music developed. Initially, they experimented with covering popular songs of the time, improvising on well-known tunes, and creating original pieces inspired by their diverse influences. The group called themselves Sigma 6 before eventually transitioning through various names, each reflecting their evolving identity and growing confidence as a musical unit.

Richard's role in the early band was primarily as a keyboardist, vocalist, and arranger. His skill on the piano and organ added depth and texture to their sound, providing a harmonic foundation that allowed Barrett's experimental guitar work and Waters' rhythmic and lyrical ideas to flourish. Richard's contributions were subtle yet essential; he had a remarkable ability to enhance a composition without overshadowing it, a trait that became a hallmark of his work throughout his career.

Early rehearsals were a laboratory for experimentation. The group explored the possibilities of electronic effects, unconventional chord progressions, and improvisational techniques. Richard, with his classical training and growing understanding of jazz and popular music, often acted as a bridge between structure and experimentation. He helped translate Barrett's abstract ideas into coherent musical arrangements, ensuring that the compositions retained emotional impact while also pushing the boundaries of traditional rock music.

Collaboration extended beyond just music. The members shared ideas about lyrics, performance style, and stage presence. They were fascinated by the possibilities of integrating visual art, sound manipulation, and theatricality into their performances. Richard, although naturally reserved, contributed thoughtfully to these discussions, providing insights that reflected both his artistic sensibility and his disciplined approach to creative problem-solving. These early collaborative experiences were crucial in shaping the dynamics of the group, establishing patterns of communication, compromise, and creative synergy that would endure through the band's evolution.

Early Musical Experiments and Performances

The early musical experiments of Richard Wright and his future bandmates were characterized by curiosity, boldness, and a willingness to challenge conventional norms. The Polytechnic environment, combined with their shared enthusiasm for avant-garde art and contemporary culture, encouraged them to explore sound in unconventional ways. They experimented with tape loops, sound effects, and electronic instruments, laying the groundwork for the atmospheric and immersive soundscapes that would later define Pink Floyd's signature style.

Richard, in particular, began experimenting with textures, layering, and the emotional use of harmony. He explored how keyboards could be used not just for melody but for atmosphere, creating moods that enhanced the overall impact of a song. His early experiments with electronic keyboards and organs allowed him to develop a distinctive sound that would later become one of the defining elements of the band's recordings.

The group began performing at small venues, local clubs, and student gatherings. These early performances were informal but critically important in developing stage presence, audience interaction, and improvisational skills. Richard's playing was often praised for its subtlety and sophistication, providing a foundation upon which Barrett's guitar and Waters' bass and vocals could interact freely. The performances were experimental, unpredictable, and electric with the energy of discovery. Each show provided lessons in collaboration, timing, and audience engagement.

Through these early musical experiments, the band began to attract attention in the London music scene. They developed a small but loyal following, drawn by their innovative sound and the originality of their compositions. For Richard, these experiences validated his commitment to music, demonstrating that his talents could flourish in a collaborative and experimental environment. The combination of disciplined musicianship, creative risk-taking, and strong interpersonal dynamics set the stage for the formation of Pink Floyd as a professional band and marked the beginning of a remarkable musical journey that would change rock history.

By the end of his time at Regent Street Polytechnic, Richard Wright had established not only his technical abilities and musical style but also his identity as a key collaborator and creative force within the emerging group. The friendships, experiments, and early performances of this period were crucial in shaping his musical philosophy, preparing him for the challenges and triumphs of a career that would redefine modern rock music. The Polytechnic years were more than an educational phase; they were the crucible in which the foundations of Pink Floyd were forged, and in which Richard Wright's quiet genius began to emerge as an indispensable element of one of the most influential bands in history.

CHAPTER 3

The Birth of Pink Floyd

The origins of Pink Floyd were humble, rooted in the experimental impulses of four young men navigating the creative currents of early 1960s London. Before the name Pink Floyd existed, the group was known as Sigma 6, a tentative project that combined shared musical interests with the casual energy of student collaboration. Sigma 6 was far from a polished ensemble. It was a space in which Roger Waters, Nick Mason, Syd Barrett, and Richard Wright could test ideas, explore instruments, and discover the dynamics of collective creation. The lineup was not rigid; it changed according to availability and interest, and the early rehearsals were as much social experiments as musical ones.

Sigma 6's repertoire consisted largely of covers of blues, rhythm and blues, and jazz standards, which gave the young musicians a foundation in structure, timing, and improvisation. These covers were important training grounds, but the group was more interested in what could be done beyond imitation. Richard Wright, with his natural facility for keyboards and his sensitivity to tonal nuance, was already experimenting with textures and harmonies that extended beyond the framework of standard pop and blues.

Even at this early stage, he demonstrated a willingness to let sounds linger, to layer chords in ways that suggested atmosphere over showmanship. This approach set him apart from many contemporaries and hinted at the sonic direction the band would later embrace.

The transition from Sigma 6 to Pink Floyd occurred gradually and was inspired by a combination of ambition and the desire for a distinct identity. Syd Barrett's growing interest in surrealism and abstract concepts for lyrics and composition prompted the group to reconsider not only their name but their artistic purpose. The name Pink Floyd itself emerged from an inventive amalgamation of the first names of two blues musicians, Pink Anderson and Floyd Council. This choice reflected both Barrett's whimsical creativity and the group's connection to the blues roots that had initially brought them together. The name also signified a break from imitation toward originality, a statement that they were intent on forging a sound and vision unique to themselves.

By the time the group had settled on Pink Floyd, they had already begun experimenting with nontraditional song structures, tape effects, and early forms of electronic manipulation. Richard Wright's keyboard work became central in this phase, as the band sought to differentiate their sound from other London-based groups. While Barrett provided a melodic anchor and Waters introduced thematic and narrative ideas, Wright created the sonic landscapes that allowed these elements to breathe. His use of organ, electric piano, and early synthesizers provided texture and depth, laying the groundwork for the immersive sound that would define the band's signature style.

Early gigs, first recordings, and initial audience reception

Pink Floyd's early gigs were modest yet electrifying laboratories for experimentation. Their first performances took place in small London clubs, at student parties, and in unconventional venues where the audience was both curious and permissive. These spaces were far from glamorous; they were often cramped, poorly lit, and acoustically challenging. Yet they provided the ideal environment for a band still learning to navigate live performance and the unpredictable dynamics of audience response.

The first recordings, though primitive by later standards, captured the raw creativity of the band. Early demos were made in makeshift studios, sometimes in friends' basements or rented rehearsal spaces. These recordings revealed a young group grappling with texture, timing, and experimentation. Richard Wright's keyboards stood out even in these early sessions, providing an emotional anchor that helped unify otherwise loosely structured pieces. While Barrett's guitar lines and Waters' lyrical sketches attracted immediate attention for their inventiveness, it was Wright's harmonic framework and vocal support that gave the music cohesion.

Audience reception was varied but generally encouraging. Some listeners were puzzled by the unconventional sounds, by tape effects, echoing vocals, and the extended instrumental passages that deviated from typical pop song structures. Others, especially younger, more open-minded fans, were captivated by the atmospheric qualities and the immersive experience the band created. These reactions reinforced the band's confidence that their approach, though unconventional, had the potential to resonate. Live performance taught them essential lessons about pacing, dynamic contrast, and the interplay between audience expectation and artistic exploration. Richard Wright, attuned to the subtleties of both sound and listener response, often adjusted his parts in real time, providing color, mood, and tension precisely where it was needed.

The band also experimented with light shows and visual elements during performances, recognizing the potential of multi-sensory experiences. Richard's melodic and harmonic contributions were complemented by projected images, swirling lights, and improvisational feedback loops. These innovations were not mere decoration. They were an integral part of creating a distinctive identity for Pink Floyd, emphasizing atmosphere over virtuosity and cohesion over flashiness. Audiences who encountered these early shows often described a feeling of being transported, of entering a soundscape rather than merely listening to a song. These responses validated the experimental direction that Wright and his bandmates were pursuing.

Richard's role as keyboardist and vocalist in shaping the band's sound

From the earliest days of Pink Floyd, Richard Wright's role extended far beyond that of a conventional keyboardist. His contributions were central to the band's ability to construct immersive, emotionally resonant music. Wright's harmonic sensibilities allowed him to create environments in which melodies and rhythms could interact in subtle and innovative ways. Unlike a soloist who dominates attention, Wright's playing emphasized atmosphere, layering, and mood. This approach distinguished him from contemporaries and made him indispensable to the band's evolving identity.

Vocally, Wright added both lead and harmony parts, often lending a soft, ethereal quality to tracks that contrasted with the more assertive voices of Barrett and Waters. His understated singing allowed lyrics to float above his harmonic textures, creating a sense of space and depth. He understood intuitively when a vocal line needed support, and when silence could be as expressive as sound. This dual role as keyboardist and vocalist provided the band with flexibility and allowed for complex arrangements that were difficult to replicate in live settings but deeply rewarding on recordings.

Wright's experimental approach to keyboards included exploring unusual chord progressions, layering different keyboard instruments, and manipulating sound through early effects and studio techniques. He often treated the keyboard as a source of color rather than just melody or rhythm, creating atmospheres that were integral to the emotional impact of the music. Whether it was a gentle electric piano, a haunting organ, or a sparse synthesizer line, Wright's choices gave Pink Floyd its distinctive sonic fingerprint. His attention to nuance and texture allowed the band to explore contrasts between noise and silence, tension and release, minimalism and complexity.

Developing the distinctive Pink Floyd atmosphere and style

The distinctive atmosphere and style of Pink Floyd did not emerge overnight. It was the product of countless experiments, rehearsals, and performances in which the members learned to balance innovation with cohesion. Richard Wright played a key role in this process. His understanding of harmony and mood enabled the band to create music that felt both expansive and intimate, structured and improvisational. Wright's keyboards were the glue that held together the other elements: Barrett's quirky guitar, Waters' thematic lyrics, and Mason's steady percussion. His sound provided the emotional contour of early songs and helped establish a vocabulary of space and color that the band would continue to refine.

The early Pink Floyd sound was characterized by fluid textures, extended instrumental passages, and an emphasis on mood over conventional song structures. Wright's influence was particularly evident in the way melodies were supported by harmonic landscapes that gave each piece a sense of journey and depth. Rather than dominating with technical flashiness, he preferred subtlety, creating layers that revealed themselves over time and rewarded careful listening. This approach encouraged the other members to explore freely, knowing that Wright would provide a cohesive underpinning that allowed risk-taking without chaos.

Atmosphere was further enhanced by Wright's attention to dynamics and pacing. He understood that tension and release were crucial, that silence could heighten emotional impact, and that a sustained chord or gentle arpeggio could carry as much weight as a melodic hook. These sensibilities were critical to the band's ability to stand apart from other groups of the time. While many bands emphasized immediate energy and catchy refrains, Pink Floyd under Wright's harmonic guidance prioritized immersive experience and emotional resonance. This distinctive approach attracted listeners who sought more than surface-level entertainment, cultivating a dedicated following that would grow over time.

Additionally, Wright's collaboration with Barrett and Waters in the studio fostered innovation in song structure and recording techniques. He was open to experimentation, willing to layer multiple keyboard parts, and capable of adapting his playing to unconventional ideas. He often contributed to arrangements, determining where textures should thicken or thin, how motifs should recur, and how passages could be interwoven for maximum impact. His aesthetic choices were subtle but crucial, giving the band the ability to craft music that felt intentional, immersive, and emotionally layered.

CHAPTER 4

Early Albums and Musical Growth

Richard Wright's contributions to Pink Floyd's debut album, The Piper at the Gates of Dawn, released in 1967, were both substantial and transformative. At this stage, the band was firmly rooted in the London underground music scene, influenced by psychedelic culture, avant-garde art, and experimental sound techniques. Wright's keyboard work became an essential element of the album, shaping its atmosphere and providing harmonic and melodic foundations that allowed the other instruments and vocals to flourish.

On The Piper at the Gates of Dawn, Richard employed a combination of piano, Farfisa organ, and other keyboard instruments to create textures that were innovative for the time. The album featured extended instrumental passages, experimental tonal shifts, and unconventional song structures. Richard's understanding of chord progressions and his improvisational skill allowed him to fill spaces with melodic lines and atmospheric layers that enhanced the experimental nature of the music. His keyboard playing often carried the emotional weight of the tracks, providing moods ranging from whimsical to mysterious, sometimes even surreal, aligning perfectly with the lyrical and conceptual content created by Syd Barrett.

Richard's approach was not merely technical; it was deeply musical and highly intuitive. For example, in tracks like "Astronomy Domine," his organ lines created an otherworldly soundscape that framed Barrett's guitar work and vocals. The layering of keyboards with the band's rhythm section allowed Pink Floyd to achieve a sound that was simultaneously psychedelic, cohesive, and innovative. His contributions were critical to the album's identity, helping the band establish a distinctive voice in a music scene that was rapidly evolving and highly competitive.

Beyond instrumentation, Richard also played a role in vocal arrangements on the album. His harmonies and background vocals added depth and texture to songs, reinforcing the ethereal qualities that became synonymous with Pink Floyd's early sound. This combination of instrumental proficiency, compositional insight, and subtle vocal layering made him an indispensable member of the band during this formative period. The debut album, while primarily associated with Barrett's creativity, owed much of its atmospheric complexity to Wright's disciplined, imaginative, and sensitive musicianship.

Musical Experimentation and Development of the Psychedelic Sound

The release of The Piper at the Gates of Dawn marked a turning point not only for Pink Floyd but for Richard Wright personally, as it allowed him to explore musical experimentation in unprecedented ways. Psychedelic rock demanded a new approach to sound, texture, and composition, and Richard's classical training and jazz influences provided him with a unique toolkit. He embraced experimentation with timbre, modulation, and electronic effects, pushing the boundaries of conventional keyboard techniques.

Richard was particularly interested in creating textures that could transform the listener's perception of space and emotion within a song. Using organs, pianos, and early electronic instruments, he developed layered, atmospheric passages that contrasted with the more direct melodies and riffs of Barrett's guitar. This approach allowed Pink Floyd to create an immersive listening experience, where the keyboards functioned both as a harmonic foundation and as a vehicle for mood and narrative. Richard's experiments with sustained chords, modal scales, and unconventional progressions became a hallmark of the band's early psychedelic sound.

The experimental nature of Pink Floyd's music also extended to studio techniques. Richard was involved in manipulating tape loops, reverb, and other effects to create sounds that were ethereal, unpredictable, and immersive. He approached the studio as an instrument itself, exploring how electronic and mechanical manipulation of sound could evoke emotion and atmosphere. This willingness to experiment was a defining trait of his musicianship and positioned him as a creative force capable of translating abstract musical ideas into tangible, evocative recordings.

Richard's contributions were not limited to creating strange or unusual sounds. His experimentation was always grounded in musicality and emotional resonance. He sought to enhance the narrative or conceptual elements of each song, ensuring that the music served both the listener's experience and the band's artistic vision. The resulting psychedelic sound of The Piper at the Gates of Dawn reflected a careful balance of technical skill, creative risk-taking, and sensitivity to atmosphere, demonstrating Richard Wright's early mastery of the art of musical experimentation.

Songwriting Contributions and Solo Parts Within Early Tracks

While Syd Barrett was the principal songwriter for Pink Floyd during the early period, Richard Wright contributed both creatively and compositionally to the album. His songwriting was characterized by a focus on harmonic innovation, melodic invention, and the creation of mood. On several tracks, Richard was credited with co-writing or contributing significant musical ideas, particularly where keyboards played a central role in defining the song's identity.

Richard's solo parts on the album were particularly notable. On tracks such as "Matilda Mother" and "Chapter 24," his piano and organ lines added layers of complexity and elegance, demonstrating his ability to create melodic interest while maintaining coherence within the band's experimental framework. His solos were never purely for show; they served the songs' overall atmosphere, enhancing their emotional and narrative impact. These solos reflected both his technical proficiency and his sense of musical empathy, as he adapted his playing to the needs of each composition.

In addition to solos, Richard often developed introductions, interludes, and transitions that tied songs together. His approach was subtle but essential, helping the album achieve a sense of cohesion despite its wide-ranging experimental elements. Through careful attention to dynamics, harmony, and texture, Richard shaped the listening experience, ensuring that the music could guide the listener through the psychedelic landscapes that Barrett and the rest of the band envisioned.

Richard's songwriting contributions also reflected his interest in melody and musical form. Unlike some members who focused primarily on lyrics or rhythm, Richard approached composition with a dual focus on structure and atmosphere. This approach allowed him to enhance Barrett's ideas, fill gaps in arrangements, and create songs that were both innovative and musically satisfying. His early compositional work laid the groundwork for later contributions, demonstrating an emerging voice that would continue to grow in sophistication and influence over the band's subsequent albums.

Relationship Dynamics Within the Band During Early Years

The early years of Pink Floyd were marked by a combination of creativity, camaraderie, and tension, as the personalities and ambitions of the members began to interact. Richard Wright, with his calm, introspective nature, often acted as a stabilizing force within the group. He provided both emotional support and musical guidance, helping the band navigate the challenges of experimentation, performance, and recording.

Richard's relationship with Syd Barrett was particularly significant. Barrett's genius and unpredictability created a dynamic that was both inspiring and challenging. Richard learned to adapt to Barrett's moods, translating the guitarist's abstract ideas into coherent musical arrangements. His patience and musical intuition allowed the band to harness Barrett's creativity without descending into chaos, ensuring that the early albums could be both experimental and listenable.

Interactions with Roger Waters and Nick Mason were characterized by mutual respect and complementary skill sets. Waters' conceptual focus and lyrical intensity found a natural balance in Richard's harmonic and atmospheric sensibilities. Mason's rhythmic inventiveness paired with Richard's melodic and textural contributions, creating a cohesive musical dialogue. Together, the four members navigated the pressures of early success, frequent performances, and the challenges of recording in a rapidly evolving music industry.

At the same time, tensions occasionally arose. Differences in personality, artistic vision, and work habits could create friction during rehearsals and studio sessions. Richard's diplomatic nature and focus on musical integrity often helped to mediate these tensions, allowing the band to maintain a collaborative spirit even during challenging periods. His ability to listen, adapt, and contribute constructively became a key factor in sustaining the group's cohesion during these formative years.

The early dynamics of Pink Floyd also reflected a broader cultural moment in London, where experimentation, individuality, and artistic risk-taking were highly valued. Richard's calm, reflective presence allowed the band to engage in these risks thoughtfully, ensuring that innovation was guided by musicality rather than chaos. This balance of experimentation, collaboration, and personal integrity laid the foundation for the band's later successes and established

Richard Wright as both a central creative force and a stabilizing influence within the group.

CHAPTER 5

Breakthrough with Dark Side of the Moon

By the early 1970s, Pink Floyd had already established themselves as innovators of progressive and psychedelic rock, yet they were still searching for a project that could unify their experimental tendencies with thematic coherence. That project arrived with The Dark Side of the Moon, released in 1973. Conceived as a concept album exploring human experience, including themes of conflict, mortality, time, and mental health, it marked a turning point in the band's creative trajectory. Richard Wright's contributions during both the writing and recording phases were essential to shaping the sound, mood, and structure of the album.

The writing process began with extensive jam sessions, where the band explored musical motifs and thematic ideas. These sessions often took place in a combination of rehearsal spaces and Abbey Road Studios, and they were characterized by a highly collaborative atmosphere. Wright's keyboard skills were central during this stage. He could quickly translate abstract concepts into musical sketches, creating harmonic frameworks that allowed other band members to experiment freely. For example, during early discussions of The Great Gig in the Sky, Wright developed chord progressions and textures that provided the dramatic and ethereal backdrop for Clare Torry's vocal performance. Similarly, on Us and Them, his use of electric piano established the song's hauntingly spacious and reflective tone. Wright's understanding of dynamics, atmosphere, and timing allowed these sketches to evolve into fully realized compositions.

The band approached the recording process with meticulous attention to detail. Each instrument was considered for both its sonic characteristics and its emotional impact. Wright experimented extensively with Hammond organ, Farfisa organ, piano, and early synthesizers such as the EMS VCS 3. His goal was to create textures that could support lyrics and melodies while simultaneously enriching the overall soundscape. He would layer multiple keyboard tracks, manipulating tone, sustain, and resonance to craft immersive sonic environments. Wright's contributions were not limited to melody; he also focused on creating a sense of space and depth, using keyboards to fill in the emotional contours of each song. This attention to harmonic and tonal detail became one of the defining features of the album.

Recording sessions were intense and precise. Engineer Alan Parsons worked closely with the band to capture subtle nuances in performance and to explore innovative studio techniques. Wright embraced these opportunities, often suggesting approaches to microphone placement, tape manipulation, or electronic processing that could enhance the emotional and spatial qualities of the music. He understood that the studio itself was an instrument and that creativity extended beyond the performance of notes into the manipulation of sound. These sessions demanded both technical skill and patience, as the band sought to achieve the perfect balance between experimental freedom and sonic clarity.

Richard's keyboard work on tracks like The Great Gig in the Sky and Us and Them

Richard Wright's keyboard contributions on The Dark Side of the Moon were essential to the album's identity. On The Great Gig in the Sky, he created the harmonic landscape over which Clare Torry's improvised vocals soared. His choice of chord voicings, sustained pads, and subtle shifts in tonal color produced a sense of anticipation, release, and transcendence. The keyboards carried the song through its narrative arc, building tension and space in parallel with the vocal line. Wright's sensitivity to dynamics allowed him to anticipate Torry's phrasing, responding with gentle flourishes and harmonic cues that enhanced the song's emotional impact.

Similarly, on Us and Them, Wright's electric piano established the song's meditative, reflective atmosphere. The repeated motifs and sustained harmonies provided a foundation for the lyrics and saxophone lines, creating a sense of both intimacy and expansiveness. Wright's playing was understated yet indispensable, demonstrating his philosophy that keyboards should support and elevate the composition rather than dominate it. He made precise decisions about timing, chord inversion, and phrasing to ensure that the instrumental texture reinforced the thematic content of the song. His contributions exemplified his ability to create aural spaces that engaged the listener on multiple levels.

Throughout the album, Wright experimented with layering multiple keyboard parts, exploring how different timbres and registers could interact to create depth and tension. For instance, on tracks such as Time and Brain Damage, his keyboards added subtle harmonic shifts, background textures, and melodic counterpoints that enriched the compositions without drawing attention away from the central themes. Wright's approach emphasized the importance of restraint and listening, as he carefully calibrated each part to complement rather than compete with the other instruments. This balance between subtlety and presence became a defining characteristic of Pink Floyd's sound during this period.

Creative process and studio innovations

The creative process for The Dark Side of the Moon was experimental, deliberate, and collaborative. Wright's role extended beyond performance to arranging, structuring, and refining ideas in the studio. He often acted as a mediator between abstract musical concepts and the technical possibilities of recording. For example, he suggested the use of tape loops, delay effects, and reverb to enhance transitions between sections and to create the feeling of continuous flow that pervades the album. His architectural sensibilities, honed during his earlier studies, allowed him to envision the album as a unified structure, with each track supporting and amplifying the others.

Innovations in the studio were central to the album's groundbreaking sound. The band experimented with quadraphonic sound, multi-track recording, and intricate layering of instruments and vocals. Wright explored ways to make the keyboard interact with tape loops and other electronic devices, producing textures that felt organic and otherworldly simultaneously. The use of early synthesizers, particularly in combination with traditional keyboard instruments, allowed Wright to create evolving soundscapes that conveyed both tension and serenity. He meticulously crafted transitions, subtle background textures, and harmonic scaffolding, all of which contributed to the sense that the album was a continuous, immersive journey rather than a collection of discrete songs.

The band's experimental ethos extended to incorporating non-musical elements into the recording. Sound effects, spoken word segments, and environmental recordings were integrated seamlessly with the keyboards and other instruments. Wright often contributed to decisions about how these elements should interact with musical parts, ensuring cohesion and balance. His contributions reflected both technical acumen and artistic intuition, demonstrating an understanding of the studio as a space for creative exploration rather than merely a place to capture live performances.

Collaboration was essential throughout the process. Wright worked closely with Parsons, Mason, Waters, and Gilmour to test ideas, refine arrangements, and troubleshoot technical challenges. His patience and meticulousness complemented the band's sometimes volatile creativity, allowing ideas to develop fully without losing focus. Wright's role in the studio underscored the importance of both musical skill and creative vision, demonstrating that the success of The Dark Side of the Moon depended not only on individual talent but on a shared commitment to experimentation and excellence.

Impact of the album on the band's career and on rock music globally

The Dark Side of the Moon represented a transformative moment for Pink Floyd. Upon its release, the album received critical acclaim for its ambition, cohesion, and innovative use of studio technology. Wright's keyboards were central to this success, providing the harmonic, textural, and emotional framework that allowed the album's themes to resonate deeply with listeners. The commercial impact was equally significant. The album became a cultural phenomenon, reaching audiences far beyond the existing fan base and establishing Pink Floyd as one of the leading voices in progressive rock.

Globally, the album influenced countless musicians and bands, reshaping expectations of what rock music could accomplish both sonically and conceptually. Wright's work demonstrated the potential of keyboards as instruments capable of shaping atmosphere, guiding narrative, and conveying complex emotion. His textures, layering, and harmonic decisions became a reference point for artists exploring ambient, progressive, and experimental music. The meticulous attention to sound quality, dynamic range, and spatial effects set a new standard for studio recording, inspiring subsequent generations of producers and engineers.

For the band, the album's success created both opportunity and challenge. Wright's contributions were now recognized on an international scale, solidifying his reputation as a key creative force within Pink Floyd. At the same time, the pressures of touring, media attention, and the expectation of continued innovation created a demanding environment. Wright navigated this landscape with his characteristic calm and dedication, ensuring that his musicianship remained central to the band's evolving sound. The album also encouraged the group to pursue increasingly ambitious projects, including elaborate stage shows and conceptually integrated performances, laying the groundwork for subsequent works such as Wish You Were Here and Animals.

CHAPTER 6

Life Behind the Scenes

Richard Wright's personality within Pink Floyd was often described as gentle, introspective, and quietly observant. Unlike Roger Waters, whose commanding presence and conceptual intensity often drove the band's creative direction, or David Gilmour, whose charisma and guitar virtuosity made him a focal point on stage, Wright tended to operate in subtler, more understated ways. His reserved demeanor allowed him to contribute meaningfully without seeking the spotlight, a quality that made him both approachable and indispensable to the collective dynamics of the group.

Wright's quiet personality contrasted sharply with other members in both social and professional contexts. Waters was known for his strong opinions and tendency to assert leadership, particularly in conceptual and lyrical matters. Gilmour's stage presence and technical confidence drew attention in performance settings, while Nick Mason, as the drummer, often acted as both anchor and mediator. In this mix, Wright's role was less about domination and more about mediation, cohesion, and enhancement. His calm temperament often provided a stabilizing influence during rehearsals, recording sessions, and tours.

This contrast extended beyond personality traits into creative expression. While Waters pursued lyrical precision and thematic ambition, and Gilmour emphasized melodic and technical virtuosity, Wright focused on atmosphere, texture, and harmonic subtlety. His musical voice was understated yet essential, adding depth, color, and cohesion to the band's compositions. This dynamic often meant that Wright's contributions were not immediately visible to casual listeners but were deeply felt by those who appreciated the layers and nuances of Pink Floyd's sound.

The quieter nature of Wright's personality also influenced the band's interpersonal relationships. He tended to avoid unnecessary conflict, preferring to listen and observe rather than assert dominance. This approach allowed him to act as a mediator in tense situations and contributed to the longevity of collaborative projects. His ability to adapt to the shifting personalities and egos within the band enabled him to maintain a consistent creative presence, even during periods of tension or change.

Contributions to the Band's Arrangements and Textures

Richard Wright's influence on Pink Floyd's music extended far beyond his visible role as a keyboardist or occasional vocalist. His contributions to arrangements and textures were central to the band's identity and were particularly evident in their more complex compositions. Wright had an intuitive understanding of how sound layers could create depth and emotion, allowing him to craft parts that enhanced melodies, harmonies, and rhythmic structures without overwhelming them.

One key aspect of Wright's contribution was his skill in harmonic layering. In tracks like Shine On You Crazy Diamond and Time, Wright employed organ, piano, and synthesizer parts that intertwined with Gilmour's guitar lines and Waters' bass to create a rich, immersive sonic tapestry. These layers were often subtle but crucial, providing the emotional undercurrent that allowed the songs to resonate with listeners. Wright's careful attention to voicing and harmonic spacing ensured that the music maintained clarity even when multiple instruments were performing simultaneously.

Wright also excelled in textural experimentation. He explored the possibilities of tone, timbre, and effects to create atmospheres that were both evocative and distinctive. Using tools such as analog synthesizers, tape loops, and studio effects, Wright contributed sounds that were novel and expressive. For example, in Us and Them, the delicate electric piano textures helped convey melancholy and contemplation, while in The Great Gig in the Sky, his layered organ harmonies provided emotional depth and cohesion. Wright's ability to integrate these textures seamlessly into the compositions became a hallmark of Pink Floyd's sound, distinguishing them from contemporaries who relied more heavily on conventional rock instrumentation.

Moreover, Wright's approach to arrangement was inherently collaborative. He listened attentively to the ideas of his bandmates, adapting his parts to complement or contrast with theirs. This sensitivity allowed him to enhance the music without overpowering it, making him a crucial balancing force in the group. His understanding of dynamics, pacing, and spatial relationships within a track contributed to the cinematic quality of Pink Floyd's albums, where each instrument and sound element had a purposeful place in the overall narrative.

Balancing Personal Life with Band Commitments

Despite the demands of international touring, recording schedules, and public appearances, Richard Wright sought to maintain balance between his personal life and professional obligations. The intensity of Pink Floyd's career, particularly during the height of their success in the 1970s and 1980s, created challenges for all band members. Wright's quieter disposition allowed him to navigate these pressures with a degree of equilibrium, though it did not exempt him from the sacrifices required by such a high-profile career.

Maintaining personal relationships was one area where Wright demonstrated care and intentionality. He prioritized time with family and close friends whenever possible, recognizing the importance of grounding himself outside the pressures of the music industry. His introspective nature meant that he valued privacy, reflection, and routine, which provided a counterbalance to the chaotic demands of touring and recording. This approach helped sustain his creativity over the long term, allowing him to contribute thoughtfully to the band while avoiding burnout.

Wright's personal interests also complemented his professional life. His continued engagement with visual arts, architecture, and musical exploration beyond Pink Floyd offered creative outlets that refreshed his perspective and inspired new ideas. These activities provided both relaxation and stimulation, contributing to his capacity to remain innovative within the band. The interplay between personal fulfillment and professional contribution was a defining feature of Wright's career, enabling him to navigate the complexities of fame and artistic expectation with composure.

Touring presented particular challenges in balancing personal and professional life. Extended periods on the road required constant adaptation, including long travel, late-night performances, and the rigors of live production. Wright's methodical and disciplined approach helped him maintain focus and energy during these periods. He approached live performances with careful preparation, ensuring that his keyboard textures, arrangements, and harmonies were executed precisely, while also allowing room for improvisation and interaction with the audience. This balance of discipline and spontaneity was reflective of his overall approach to life behind the scenes.

Early Struggles with Recognition and Creative Control

Despite his substantial contributions, Richard Wright often faced struggles with recognition and creative control within Pink Floyd. His understated personality and collaborative style meant that his role was sometimes overlooked in public discussions about the band's music. Critics and audiences frequently focused on Waters' conceptual leadership or Gilmour's guitar work, while Wright's essential influence on harmonic structure, texture, and mood received less attention.

This dynamic occasionally created tension within the band, particularly when decisions regarding songwriting credits, album direction, or stage presentation were made. Wright's contributions were vital to the band's sound, but his preference for subtlety sometimes left him in the background of recognition, both internally and externally. Nevertheless, his quiet professionalism and commitment to the music allowed him to navigate these challenges without compromising the quality of his work.

Creative control was another area where Wright had to negotiate his position. The dominance of other band members in decision-making, particularly Waters during periods of conceptual focus, sometimes limited Wright's ability to assert his own artistic ideas fully. Despite this, Wright continued to innovate within his domain, using keyboards, harmonics, and arrangements to influence the overall sound of the band. His adaptability and willingness to collaborate allowed him to contribute meaningfully while managing the constraints of the band's hierarchical dynamics.

Wright's early struggles with recognition and creative control were intertwined with his personal philosophy regarding music. He valued the collective result over individual acclaim, believing that the cohesion and emotional impact of the band's output were more important than personal visibility. This approach, though it sometimes meant he received less public acknowledgment, ensured that Pink Floyd's music achieved the depth, richness, and atmospheric quality that became its hallmark. Over time, critics and fellow musicians came to recognize Wright's essential role, highlighting his contributions to the band's arrangements, textures, and distinctive soundscapes.

By maintaining composure, balancing personal and professional responsibilities, and committing to subtle but impactful contributions, Richard Wright established himself as the quiet architect of Pink Floyd's sonic identity. His ability to enhance compositions, support his bandmates, and innovate within a collaborative framework reinforced the depth and sophistication of the group's music. Life behind the scenes, while often overshadowed by more prominent personalities, was where Wright's vision, discipline, and creativity were most fully realized, shaping the band's sound in ways that would resonate across decades of music history.

CHAPTER 7

Wish You Were Here and Animals

By the mid-1970s, Pink Floyd had solidified their reputation as pioneers of progressive rock, with a unique sound shaped in large part by Richard Wright's keyboard artistry. The 1975 album Wish You Were Here represented a pivotal moment in the band's creative journey, marked by reflection, experimentation, and tribute. Wright's contributions to the album were essential both in terms of keyboard performance and compositional input, as he helped shape its atmospheric soundscapes, melodic foundations, and emotional depth.

Richard's keyboards formed the backbone of several tracks on Wish You Were Here. On the album's opening piece, Shine On You Crazy Diamond, Wright's playing was fundamental in establishing the iconic, haunting atmosphere. His piano and synthesizer textures created a sense of vastness and melancholy, perfectly complementing David Gilmour's guitar lines and Roger Waters' conceptual framework. Wright's ability to construct long, flowing chord progressions, layered with subtle harmonic shifts, allowed the band to convey deep emotional resonance without overwhelming the listener. His work was both technically sophisticated and emotionally expressive, balancing precision with intuition.

In addition to Shine On You Crazy Diamond, Wright's keyboard contributions on tracks like Welcome to the Machine and Have a Cigar further demonstrate his range and creativity. He used synthesizers, organ, and piano to produce textures that enhanced the conceptual narratives of the songs, from the alienating industrial sounds of Welcome to the Machine to the satirical tone of Have a Cigar. Wright's understanding of tonal color and mood allowed him to adapt his playing to each song's emotional requirements, contributing to the album's overall cohesion. His ability to integrate seamlessly with Gilmour's guitar and Mason's rhythmic structures was essential to the creation of the immersive soundscapes that define the record.

Moreover, Wright's compositional input extended beyond performance. He participated in arranging the tracks, suggesting structural transitions, harmonizations, and layering techniques that enhanced the dramatic impact of the music. His subtle yet decisive influence ensured that the album maintained its conceptual integrity while allowing room for improvisation and experimentation. Wright's sensitivity to dynamics, pacing, and mood created an auditory environment in which the album's themes of absence, loss, and reflection could resonate fully with listeners.

The Making of Animals and Richard's Role in Conceptual Tracks

Following the success of Wish You Were Here, Pink Floyd embarked on the creation of Animals, released in 1977. The album marked a shift toward politically charged themes, inspired by George Orwell's Animal Farm, and explored societal hierarchies, human behavior, and social critique. Richard Wright's keyboard contributions were central to the album's conceptual execution, as he provided the textures, atmospheres, and melodic structures that allowed the thematic content to unfold with clarity and impact.

Wright's approach to Animals was both technical and interpretive. On tracks such as Dogs, Pigs, and Sheep, his keyboards provided harmonic foundations that reinforced the narrative arcs of the songs. The piano and synthesizer arrangements created tension, emotional resonance, and dynamic contrast, enhancing the storytelling aspect of the album. His use of sustained chords, subtle modulations, and layered textures emphasized the complexity of the characters and situations depicted in the lyrics, adding depth to the band's exploration of societal critique.

In addition to performing, Wright played a role in the conceptual development of the tracks. His musical ideas often influenced the pacing, structure, and mood of the songs, shaping how the band communicated their thematic intentions. He contributed to the development of instrumental sections, particularly in extended passages where the music needed to convey narrative progression without relying on lyrics. Wright's understanding of emotional nuance and musical space ensured that these sections maintained coherence and engagement, reinforcing the conceptual strength of the album.

The recording process for Animals was marked by careful experimentation with sounds and textures. Wright collaborated closely with Gilmour and Mason to develop arrangements that balanced narrative clarity with musical exploration. He experimented with electronic textures, synthesizers, and effects to create moods that were dark, brooding, and reflective of the album's themes. His subtle use of timbre and harmonic layering gave the tracks a richness and depth that complemented Waters' biting lyrics, establishing an immersive listening experience.

Collaboration Challenges and Interpersonal Tensions Within the Band

While Wish You Were Here and Animals showcased Pink Floyd at the height of their creativity, these albums were also produced during periods of increasing tension and interpersonal complexity within the band. Richard Wright's quieter personality and collaborative nature often contrasted with the more dominant traits of Roger Waters and other members, creating both challenges and opportunities in the creative process.

During the recording of Animals, tensions regarding creative control became particularly pronounced. Waters, increasingly assertive in shaping the thematic and musical direction of the band, sometimes marginalized Wright's input, despite his central role in arranging and texturing the tracks. Wright's contributions, though critical to the sound and cohesion of the music, were occasionally overlooked in decision-making processes. Nevertheless, he continued to assert his influence through musical intuition, providing essential textures and arrangements that ensured the integrity of the recordings.

Richard's relationship with Gilmour remained collaborative yet complex. The two often shared responsibilities in arranging, improvising, and developing musical ideas, yet differences in approach occasionally led to friction. Wright's preference for subtle, atmospheric contributions sometimes contrasted with Gilmour's melodic assertiveness, requiring negotiation and compromise. Despite these challenges, Wright maintained a professional and constructive approach, ensuring that creative disagreements did not compromise the musical quality of the albums.

The tensions were not limited to the studio. Touring and live performances brought additional pressures, as extended periods of travel, performance expectations, and public scrutiny amplified interpersonal stress. Wright's quiet temperament allowed him to mediate conflicts and maintain focus on musical goals, serving as a stabilizing influence amidst the growing intensity of the band's internal dynamics. His capacity to navigate these challenges while continuing to contribute creatively reflects both resilience and a commitment to artistic excellence.

Highlights of Live Performances and Tours During This Era

The release of Wish You Were Here and Animals was accompanied by ambitious live performances and tours, which highlighted Richard Wright's musicianship and the band's innovative stagecraft. These tours were characterized by elaborate visual effects, extended instrumental passages, and immersive sound design, all of which relied heavily on Wright's keyboard work to maintain the musical foundation and atmosphere.

Wright's performances were marked by precision, sensitivity, and adaptability. During live renditions of tracks such as Shine On You Crazy Diamond, Dogs, and Pigs, he was responsible for recreating complex keyboard textures that had been carefully crafted in the studio. His ability to manage multiple keyboard instruments, layer sounds, and adjust dynamically to the evolving performance allowed the band to deliver immersive live experiences that retained the depth and nuance of the recordings.

These tours also provided Wright with opportunities to explore improvisation and experimentation. While the arrangements of the studio tracks were meticulously

70

prepared, live performances often required adaptation to acoustics, audience response, and technical conditions. Wright's skill in integrating improvisational elements while maintaining coherence exemplified his mastery of musical flexibility and his understanding of the live performance as a dynamic art form.

The visual and conceptual components of the tours were similarly enhanced by Wright's work. The band's use of lighting, projections, and stage design relied on the music to create atmosphere and narrative flow. Wright's textured keyboards provided the foundation for these effects, ensuring that the emotional and conceptual impact of the performances was fully realized. Audiences responded enthusiastically, recognizing the interplay between musical innovation and visual spectacle, and Wright's contributions were essential to this immersive experience.

Moreover, these tours solidified Pink Floyd's reputation as one of the most innovative live acts of the era. The combination of complex musical arrangements, technological experimentation, and conceptual storytelling demonstrated the band's commitment to pushing the boundaries of rock performance. Wright's quiet yet indispensable role in creating these experiences underscored the importance of his musicianship, highlighting his ability to shape soundscapes that were both technically sophisticated and emotionally compelling.

CHAPTER 8

Tensions and The Wall

By the late 1970s, Pink Floyd had reached the height of their commercial success, yet with this acclaim came a growing tension within the band. The creative and personal dynamics that had fueled their early innovations were beginning to show signs of strain. Roger Waters, increasingly assertive as the conceptual leader of the band, was directing the artistic vision more forcefully than ever before. He had conceived The Wall as a rock opera exploring alienation, isolation, and the psychological effects of fame, trauma, and societal pressures. This ambitious undertaking required a level of precision, focus, and narrative cohesion that inevitably intensified existing conflicts among the band members.

Richard Wright, who had always been known for his calm, introspective personality, found himself in a challenging position. His approach to music emphasized collaboration, texture, and subtlety. While he had always contributed significantly to the harmonic and atmospheric aspects of the band's sound, he was less inclined to dominate the conceptual direction of albums. Waters' increasingly unilateral decision-making created tension, as Wright's input into arrangements and song development was often overshadowed. Disagreements arose not from a lack of skill or vision on Wright's part, but from differences in leadership style, creative priorities, and interpersonal communication.

David Gilmour's emergence as a powerful guitarist and songwriter further complicated matters. Gilmour's melodic sensibility and technical expertise provided essential support for Waters' conceptual narratives, but his growing prominence sometimes relegated Wright to a secondary role. Mason, while generally more neutral, focused on rhythmic precision and technical execution rather than conceptual direction, leaving Wright and Waters to negotiate the larger artistic vision. The interplay of these personalities created an environment in which creative disagreements were frequent, communication could be strained, and collaboration was often fraught with tension.

The conflicts leading up to The Wall were both creative and personal. Waters' desire for strict adherence to his vision for the album often clashed with Wright's intuitive and exploratory approach to music. Wright sought to contribute harmonically, texturally, and atmospherically, but found his ideas minimized or redirected to serve Waters' narrative. The intensity of these conflicts was magnified by the pressure to produce a commercially successful album that could also satisfy the band's reputation for innovation. Wright's quieter temperament made it challenging to assert himself in debates dominated by stronger or more vocal personalities, resulting in feelings of frustration and marginalization.

Despite the conflicts, Wright remained committed to the band and the music. He understood the importance of maintaining cohesion and professionalism, even when personal differences threatened to derail the creative process. His ability to navigate these tensions without allowing them to disrupt the music was a testament to his maturity, resilience, and dedication. Wright's presence ensured that the harmonic richness and textural depth of Pink Floyd's sound continued to evolve, even as interpersonal dynamics became increasingly strained.

Richard's diminishing role and temporary departure

As the production of The Wall progressed, Richard Wright's role within Pink Floyd became increasingly constrained. Waters' assertive leadership meant that many decisions regarding arrangements, song structure, and conceptual focus were made without extensive consultation with Wright. While Wright remained essential to the harmonic and atmospheric qualities of the album, his creative contributions were often limited to executing parts that had already been predetermined. This shift represented a significant change from earlier projects, where Wright had played a more integrative and collaborative role in shaping the band's sound.

Faced with this diminishing influence, Wright made the difficult decision to leave the band temporarily before the subsequent tour. His departure was not born of anger or a lack of commitment but stemmed from a desire to preserve his personal and creative integrity. Wright's quiet reflection allowed him to recognize the unsustainable nature of the working environment, where his input was undervalued and tensions with Waters threatened both personal well-being and artistic fulfillment. Leaving the band provided him with space to reassess his role, consider his future, and protect his mental and emotional health in the face of intense pressure.

Despite his official departure, Wright's involvement in the album remained substantial. He completed the recording of keyboard and synthesizer parts, contributing piano, organ, and electronic textures that were integral to the final sound. Tracks such as Hey You, Comfortably Numb, and Another Brick in the Wall Part Two benefited from Wright's harmonic sensitivity and atmospheric layering, ensuring that the music retained the depth, richness, and emotional resonance characteristic of Pink Floyd. Wright's ability to contribute effectively while stepping back from the central decision-making process demonstrated both his professionalism and his commitment to the music over personal recognition.

The temporary departure also reflected broader questions about creative control and recognition within a band of strong personalities. Wright had consistently prioritized musical quality and cohesion, sometimes at the expense of asserting authority over conceptual direction. His departure highlighted the difficulties that even highly skilled and integral musicians could face when navigating hierarchical dynamics, particularly when a single member exerts significant influence over the artistic and managerial aspects of a project.

Session work and touring contributions despite internal struggles

Even after officially leaving the band, Richard Wright continued to contribute as a session musician and live performer. His keyboard work was essential in translating the intricate studio arrangements of The Wall into a live setting, ensuring that the complex textures, harmonic nuances, and atmospheric effects were faithfully represented on stage. Wright's ability to maintain precision and expressive depth during live performances underscored his technical mastery and professional discipline, even under emotionally challenging circumstances.

The Wall tour was among the most ambitious and logistically complex in rock history. The stage design featured elaborate constructions, including the literal wall itself, extensive visual projections, puppetry, and intricate lighting. Wright's keyboard textures were critical in maintaining continuity and cohesion amid these theatrical elements. His piano and synthesizer parts provided harmonic support and melodic embellishment, allowing Gilmour's guitar and Mason's percussion to interact with Waters' narrative and vocal performances seamlessly. Wright's contributions ensured that the immersive, cinematic experience of The Wall was not only visually compelling but also musically precise and emotionally engaging.

Recording sessions for the album also required Wright to adapt to a reduced role while maintaining high standards of musicianship. He executed complex parts that demanded technical precision and emotional nuance, working within Waters' conceptual framework while subtly infusing his own musical sensibility. His disciplined approach and attention to detail ensured that his keyboard lines enhanced the narrative and emotional impact of each track without challenging the overarching vision dictated by Waters. This balancing act required both humility and confidence, as Wright contributed meaningfully while accepting constraints on creative control.

Throughout this period, Wright demonstrated resilience and adaptability. Despite the strain of diminished recognition and creative authority, he remained committed to excellence in performance and recording. His work was essential in preserving the distinctive Pink Floyd sound, ensuring that The Wall maintained the harmonic depth, textural richness, and emotional resonance that audiences expected from the band. Wright's contributions during this era exemplify the role of a musician whose impact is measured not only by visibility or leadership but by consistency, skill, and thoughtful artistry.

Reflections on creative differences and personal growth

The experience of producing and performing The Wall provided Richard Wright with profound insights into creative collaboration, personal resilience, and artistic identity. Navigating diminished authority, interpersonal tension, and the demands of large-scale production forced him to reflect deeply on his role within the band and the nature of artistic contribution. Wright recognized that influence in a collaborative environment does not always correlate with visibility or decision-making power; it can reside in the quality, consistency, and nuance of one's contributions.

These challenges fostered personal growth. Wright developed strategies to maintain his artistic integrity while working within a structure dominated by a strong-willed conceptual leader. He honed the ability to contribute harmonically, texturally, and atmospherically without confrontation, finding ways to infuse his personality into the music subtly but effectively. This period strengthened his emotional intelligence, patience, and strategic thinking, skills that would serve him in future collaborations both within and outside Pink Floyd.

The tensions and constraints of this era also prompted Wright to consider alternative avenues for creative expression. While his role within the band was temporarily limited, he recognized the importance of pursuing individual projects, exploring new musical ideas, and maintaining personal creative space. These reflections informed his subsequent decisions to rejoin the band under more favorable conditions and to develop solo projects that allowed him to explore his musical identity more fully.

CHAPTER 9

Solo Work and Personal Projects

After the tensions and challenges surrounding The Wall, Richard Wright felt a pressing need to rediscover his own musical voice. For years, Wright's contributions to Pink Floyd had been essential to the band's signature sound, yet often subtle and understated. He provided the harmonic foundation, textural layering, and atmospheric color that elevated the band's compositions, but much of his creative identity was intertwined with the collective output of the group. The opportunity to create a solo album allowed him to explore a musical path unmediated by the demands of collaboration and hierarchy. This opportunity became realized with the release of Wet Dream in 1978, an album that marked Wright's emergence as an independent artist capable of expressing his personal musical vision.

Wet Dream represented both experimentation and introspection. Wright approached it as a canvas for exploring melodic, harmonic, and textural ideas that had long been constrained by the priorities of Pink Floyd. Unlike the grand concept albums of the band, the album emphasized mood, tone, and nuance. Wright's careful attention to composition was evident in the layering of keyboards, the interplay of piano and synthesizer, and the integration of subtle percussive elements. His work demonstrated a refined understanding of how harmonic structure could evoke emotional responses without requiring overtly dramatic gestures. The album's compositions were deliberate, flowing with a quiet confidence that reflected Wright's introspective approach to music-making.

The creation of Wet Dream allowed Wright to explore different aspects of his musicianship. He was able to perform multiple instruments on the album, including piano, Hammond organ, synthesizers, and even occasional guitar lines. This autonomy gave him complete control over the sound and structure of each piece. The compositions reveal his interest in blending genres, with elements of jazz, classical piano techniques, and soft rock harmoniously integrated. This integration reflected Wright's lifelong fascination with texture and mood, demonstrating how he could sustain listener interest through subtle harmonic shifts, dynamic interplay, and carefully orchestrated instrumental layers.

Wet Dream also reflected Wright's personal journey. The album's reflective nature suggested a musician reconsidering his place within the music world, confronting the challenge of stepping out of the collective identity of Pink Floyd and embracing a solo voice. Each track carried a sense of quiet exploration, signaling a willingness to experiment with tonal colors, sonic textures, and melodic phrasing. Wright was not attempting to create a commercial blockbuster but rather an intimate statement of artistic identity, highlighting his compositional skill and harmonic sensitivity. In this sense, Wet Dream was a declaration of independence, demonstrating that Wright's artistry extended far beyond the boundaries of the band he had helped define.

Musical Style, Themes, and Reception of His Solo Albums

Richard Wright's solo musical style was characterized by harmonic sophistication, atmospheric layering, and a focus on melodic subtlety. Unlike Pink Floyd, where albums were often concept-driven and narrative-heavy, his solo work prioritized texture and mood over storyline or spectacle. Wright consistently demonstrated an acute sense of timing, dynamic balance, and spatial arrangement in his compositions, producing music that was immersive and emotionally resonant. The tracks often carried a contemplative tone, inviting listeners into reflective, meditative spaces rather than demanding attention through dramatic shifts or complex conceptual frameworks.

Themes in Wright's solo albums frequently centered on introspection, personal reflection, and emotional landscapes. While Pink Floyd addressed social, political, and psychological themes on a grand scale, Wright's solo work offered intimate explorations of human emotion, vulnerability, and the experience of solitude. Through his compositions, he conveyed feelings of melancholy, serenity, and subtle tension, using harmonic progression and textural layering to create an emotional narrative. The contemplative nature of his music invited listeners to engage deeply, appreciating the understated beauty of chordal interplay and ambient color.

The reception of Wright's solo albums was mixed, reflecting the challenges of separating individual achievement from the collective identity of Pink Floyd. Critics often recognized the elegance, harmonic depth, and textural richness of Wet Dream and subsequent solo efforts, noting Wright's skill as a keyboardist and composer. However, comparisons to Pink Floyd's landmark albums sometimes overshadowed the subtler achievements of his solo work. Some listeners found the albums understated, lacking the grandiose spectacle they associated with the band. Nevertheless, his solo work established him as an artist of subtlety and refinement, capable of crafting music that was technically sophisticated, emotionally resonant, and harmonically compelling.

Musically, Wright continued to experiment with synthesizers and electronic instruments, expanding his tonal palette and embracing new technologies. His solo albums demonstrate an evolving understanding of electronic sound design, ambient layering, and the spatial deployment of instruments within a composition. This experimentation not only enhanced the textural quality of his solo music but also informed his later work with Pink Floyd, where he integrated new sonic ideas into the band's evolving sound. Wright's solo style reflects a balance between discipline and exploration, structure and improvisation, demonstrating his capacity to innovate while maintaining musical coherence.

Collaborations Outside of Pink Floyd

During his time away from full involvement with Pink Floyd, Richard Wright engaged in collaborations with other musicians and projects, further broadening his musical horizons. These collaborations ranged from studio sessions to co-writing arrangements for other artists, providing opportunities to experiment with new ideas in environments less constrained by the expectations and hierarchies of his band. Wright's expertise in keyboards, harmonic layering, and atmospheric design made him a valuable collaborator, particularly for projects requiring subtle textural contributions rather than dominant melodic or rhythmic focus.

Collaborations allowed Wright to explore musical genres and techniques that differed from the progressive rock context of Pink Floyd. He worked with jazz-influenced projects, ambient soundscapes, and other experimental recordings, bringing his harmonic sensibility and refined keyboard skills to each endeavor. These experiences helped Wright develop versatility, adaptability, and a more nuanced understanding of musical collaboration, exposing him to diverse approaches to composition, production, and instrumentation. By working outside the familiar band framework, Wright was able to test new ideas, refine his technical abilities, and cultivate creative independence.

The collaborative experiences also strengthened Wright's professional skills, teaching him how to integrate his contributions into other artists' visions while maintaining his own musical identity. He learned to balance assertiveness and sensitivity, to recognize where his influence could enhance a project, and to adjust his approach based on the goals, styles, and expectations of collaborators. These lessons enriched his understanding of musical leadership, teamwork, and creative negotiation, preparing him to reintegrate into Pink Floyd with renewed confidence and broader experience.

Wright's external collaborations also helped solidify his reputation as a musician of integrity, sophistication, and subtlety. While he was not seeking the spotlight, his work was respected for its intelligence, sensitivity, and emotional impact. Collaborators valued his ability to enrich compositions without overshadowing them, demonstrating the quiet authority of an artist confident in his skills but unassuming in demeanor. These projects highlighted Wright's versatility and reinforced his status as a creative force capable of contributing meaningfully in multiple musical contexts.

Lessons Learned from Working Independently

Richard Wright's period of solo work and independent collaboration provided profound lessons in artistry, self-discipline, and creative identity. Managing a solo album required him to make decisions on composition, instrumentation, arrangement, and production independently. This responsibility taught him to trust his instincts, refine his sense of musical judgment, and develop a disciplined approach to problem-solving in the creative process. Wright gained a deeper understanding of how to construct cohesive musical statements, balancing melody, texture, and harmonic complexity without relying on external input.

Working independently also reinforced the importance of patience, attention to detail, and subtlety in musical communication. Wright realized that impact does not always require dramatic gestures; carefully crafted harmonic progressions, layered textures, and thoughtfully applied dynamics can create profound emotional resonance. This understanding deepened his artistic maturity, emphasizing that effective musicianship is as much about restraint and refinement as it is about technical virtuosity or conceptual ambition.

Another critical lesson was the value of self-reliance balanced with humility. Wright learned to assert his musical ideas while recognizing the necessity of adapting to technical constraints, production realities, and listener expectations. This balance of confidence and sensitivity became a guiding principle in his later work, enabling him to contribute to Pink Floyd with a stronger sense of purpose and clarity. Working independently also offered insight into the dynamics of creative collaboration, highlighting the differences between leadership, negotiation, and supportive artistry.

Finally, Wright's solo projects demonstrated that creative fulfillment can exist outside of large-scale recognition or commercial success. While his solo albums did not achieve the same fame as Pink Floyd releases, they provided personal satisfaction, artistic growth, and technical development. The experience strengthened his identity as a musician capable of standing independently, reinforcing both his confidence and his long-term commitment to musical exploration. These lessons informed his reintegration into Pink Floyd, where he brought a renewed sense of agency, creative insight, and a broadened perspective on musical collaboration.

CHAPTER 10

Return to Pink Floyd

After several years of pursuing solo projects and exploring personal musical ventures, Richard Wright returned to Pink Floyd during the production of A Momentary Lapse of Reason in the late 1980s. The band had undergone a dramatic transformation since the departure of Roger Waters, whose exit left both creative and managerial gaps. David Gilmour and Nick Mason were determined to continue the legacy of Pink Floyd while redefining the band's dynamics. They recognized that Wright's harmonic sophistication, textural expertise, and subtle atmospheric contributions were essential for preserving the distinctive Pink Floyd sound. Inviting Wright back was both a strategic and symbolic decision, aiming to restore the musical depth that had been diminished in his absence.

Wright's return was initially as a session musician rather than a full band member, due to contractual complexities and the transitional state of the group. Despite this limited official status, his contributions were central to the album. He played keyboards, synthesizers, piano, and provided backing vocals, establishing the harmonic and atmospheric foundations for tracks that needed to blend the traditional

Pink Floyd style with a contemporary sound. Songs like On the Turning Away and Learning to Fly relied heavily on his layered keyboard textures and melodic subtlety. Wright's involvement helped maintain continuity with Pink Floyd's earlier works, creating a sonic bridge between the classic progressive rock albums and this new era.

Rejoining the band required Wright to navigate altered interpersonal dynamics. Having been absent during the Wall era and its ensuing conflicts, he faced the challenge of reintegrating into a band where power structures and creative responsibilities had shifted. Wright approached this challenge with his characteristic calm, patience, and professionalism. He maintained a focus on the music rather than personal politics, allowing him to reintegrate smoothly and contribute meaningfully to both recording and arrangement processes. This approach reflected his growth as an artist, demonstrating both maturity and strategic understanding of the collaborative process.

The recording of A Momentary Lapse of Reason also demanded Wright to adapt to technological advancements in the studio. The 1980s saw a significant expansion in the use of digital synthesizers, sequencers, and recording techniques. Wright embraced these tools, integrating modern sounds with his traditional piano and organ textures. His ability to blend acoustic and electronic elements seamlessly enriched the album's sonic depth and preserved the band's hallmark atmospheric quality. Wright's return marked a balance between continuity and innovation, allowing Pink Floyd to evolve musically without losing its foundational identity.

Role in The Division Bell and Reunion Dynamics

Following the relative success of A Momentary Lapse of Reason, Wright's involvement in Pink Floyd deepened with The Division Bell, released in 1994. By this time, he was recognized as a full contributing member rather than a session musician, and his creative input played a critical role in shaping the album's sound. The Division Bell was a project that emphasized collaboration and refinement, relying heavily on Wright's harmonic sensibilities, textural layering, and melodic intuition. His keyboard work became central to songs like High Hopes, Marooned, and Keep Talking, where his atmospheric textures, ambient chords, and subtle melodic embellishments enhanced the overall sonic landscape.

The reunion dynamics during The Division Bell era were markedly different from previous decades. The absence of Roger Waters eliminated the intense power struggles and conceptual dominance that had previously constrained Wright's contributions. David Gilmour's leadership style was more inclusive, allowing Wright and Mason to influence arrangements, textural decisions, and harmonization. Wright's return facilitated a more balanced, collaborative environment, where his musical ideas were recognized and integrated rather than minimized. This environment allowed Wright to assert his artistry while maintaining the supportive, integrative role he had always excelled at.

The Division Bell also represented an era of musical maturity for Wright. His prior experience with solo projects and collaborations had expanded his technical expertise and artistic perspective. He applied these insights to the album, experimenting with new keyboard textures, synthesizer timbres, and ambient layering techniques. The result was a sound that was both contemporary and reminiscent of classic Pink Floyd, achieving a balance that satisfied both long-time fans and new audiences. Wright's contributions were essential in creating the spacious, reflective, and immersive atmosphere that defined the album, reaffirming his importance as a creative architect within the band.

Contributions to Live Tours and Recordings

Richard Wright's role in Pink Floyd's live performances during this period was equally vital. The tours for both A Momentary Lapse of Reason and The Division Bell were logistically complex and musically demanding. Wright played keyboards, piano, and synthesizers, recreating the intricate studio arrangements in a live context. His presence was essential for maintaining the harmonic richness and textural depth that were the hallmarks of Pink Floyd's sound. Live tracks such as Shine On You Crazy Diamond, Wish You Were Here, and Comfortably Numb demanded precision and subtlety, both of which Wright delivered consistently.

Live performances in this era were highly elaborate, incorporating sophisticated lighting, projections, and stage designs. Wright's keyboard parts often synchronized with visual elements, requiring careful timing and adaptability. His ability to remain focused under these conditions highlighted his professionalism and mastery of live performance. He also contributed backing vocals and melodic embellishments, reinforcing the band's layered harmonies and enhancing the audience's experience. The live tours showcased not only his technical skill but also his musical intuition, as he balanced the demands of faithful reproduction with spontaneous expressive adjustments to suit the live environment.

In addition to live performance, Wright's studio contributions during this period remained significant. On The Division Bell, his keyboard textures were integral to both melodic and atmospheric development. He employed a variety of instruments and techniques, from acoustic piano to digital synthesizers, creating layers that added depth, warmth, and complexity. Wright's understanding of spatial arrangement, harmonic progression, and tonal layering ensured that the album retained Pink Floyd's signature immersive quality. His contributions were collaborative yet distinctive, blending seamlessly with Gilmour's guitar, Mason's percussion, and the other studio elements to produce a cohesive, polished final product.

Wright's adaptability extended to evolving musical technologies. By the 1990s, recording practices had shifted significantly toward digital processing, multi-track layering, and synthesized sound design. Wright's willingness to embrace these changes while maintaining the integrity of his melodic and harmonic sensibilities allowed him to remain a key contributor to both studio and live works. His ability to balance innovation with tradition was crucial for sustaining the band's identity while adapting to contemporary musical landscapes.

Regaining Recognition and Respect Within the Band

One of the most significant aspects of Wright's return was the restoration of recognition and respect within Pink Floyd. During earlier periods, particularly the Wall era, Wright had experienced marginalization. Despite his essential contributions, his role was often diminished by dominant personalities and hierarchical decision-making. Returning to the band allowed him to reclaim his position as a respected creative partner. His technical expertise, harmonic insight, and melodic intuition were recognized as central to the integrity of the band's sound.

The renewed respect for Wright was evident in the recording sessions, where his ideas for texture, harmony, and arrangement were actively solicited and integrated. David Gilmour and Nick Mason valued Wright's experience, subtlety, and musical intelligence, creating an environment where his contributions were no longer overshadowed. Wright's artistic voice became a vital part of the band's evolving sound, influencing both composition and performance. His restored role demonstrated that influence in a creative environment is not only about prominence but also about the consistent quality and sensitivity of one's work.

Wright's personal and professional growth during his solo years contributed to the renewed recognition he received. He returned with confidence, technical skill, and an expanded artistic perspective. He was able to assert his creative vision while maintaining the collaborative ethos of the band. This maturity allowed him to navigate the complexities of group dynamics effectively, balancing leadership, collaboration, and supportive musicianship. His restored recognition was a testament to both his talent and his resilience, affirming his essential role in sustaining Pink Floyd's legacy.

His contributions also reinforced the importance of subtlety in musical collaboration. Wright's ability to enhance the work of others without dominating it demonstrated the quiet power of thoughtful musicianship. Through his keyboards, harmonic layers, and ambient textures, he enriched the emotional and sonic landscape of Pink Floyd's music. The respect he regained was both personal and professional, reflecting acknowledgment of his artistic authority, technical skill, and enduring influence on the band's sound.

CHAPTER 11

Musical Style and Legacy

Richard Wright's signature sound was defined by a combination of subtlety, harmonic sophistication, and a mastery of keyboard textures that created the distinctive atmosphere of Pink Floyd's music. His approach to keyboards was not merely about playing notes or providing accompaniment; it was about crafting immersive sonic landscapes that enhanced the emotional and conceptual content of the compositions. Wright's understanding of tone, chord voicing, and spatial placement within arrangements was central to the band's identity and distinguished him as one of rock's most innovative keyboardists.

One of Wright's most notable techniques was his use of layered keyboards to create depth and texture. He often combined piano, Hammond organ, Farfisa organ, and synthesizers to build multi-dimensional soundscapes. By carefully balancing the timbres of each instrument, he could create lush harmonies and ethereal backgrounds without overcrowding the arrangement. His use of sustained chords, modal shifts, and contrapuntal lines allowed him to fill sonic space in ways that were both subtle and powerful, providing an emotional framework for Gilmour's guitar solos and Waters' bass lines.

Wright was also a pioneer in synthesizer techniques within rock music. He utilized analog synthesizers, such as the EMS VCS 3 and ARP String Ensemble, to produce textures that ranged from haunting and atmospheric to vibrant and dynamic. His approach emphasized modulation, layering, and real-time manipulation of sound parameters, allowing him to respond to the evolving mood of a song. For example, in tracks like On the Run and Shine On You Crazy Diamond, Wright's synthesizers added movement, tension, and ethereal coloration, effectively bridging the gap between traditional keyboard sounds and futuristic sonic experimentation.

Additionally, Wright's melodic sensibility was integral to his signature sound. Unlike many rock keyboardists of the era who focused on flashy solos or virtuosic displays, Wright favored melodic lines that complemented and enhanced the overall composition. His counter-melodies, fills, and harmonic underpinnings provided emotional resonance and structural cohesion. Whether playing subtle arpeggios in Us and Them or sustaining ethereal pads in Echoes, Wright demonstrated an intuitive understanding of how keyboards could shape the listener's experience without dominating the sonic landscape.

Another hallmark of Wright's technique was his use of space and dynamics. He understood the importance of silence, restraint, and timing in musical expression. By strategically placing notes, chords, and textures, he created tension, anticipation, and release, adding narrative depth to songs. This mastery of dynamics allowed Pink Floyd's music to achieve its cinematic quality, where every instrument and sound served a purposeful role in constructing immersive atmospheres.

Influence on Pink Floyd's Overall Style and Rock Music

Richard Wright's influence on Pink Floyd's overall style cannot be overstated. His harmonic sensibilities, textural layering, and emotional phrasing were central to the band's identity, shaping their evolution from psychedelic pioneers to progressive rock innovators and beyond. Wright's keyboards provided a sonic glue that connected disparate musical elements, allowing Pink Floyd to create albums that were cohesive, immersive, and conceptually unified.

Wright's contributions were especially critical in defining the band's approach to atmosphere and mood. Whereas Waters often focused on lyrical content and conceptual framing, and Gilmour on melodic and guitar virtuosity, Wright's work provided the emotional and harmonic foundation that allowed these elements to resonate fully. His keyboards created a sense of space, depth, and continuity, enabling Pink Floyd to explore long-form compositions, complex arrangements, and thematic albums without losing coherence.

Beyond Pink Floyd, Wright's influence extended to rock music more broadly. His pioneering use of synthesizers and layered keyboard textures inspired subsequent generations of musicians to explore ambient, progressive, and electronic approaches within rock and beyond. Bands in the progressive rock movement, ambient music circles, and modern electronic rock often cite Wright's approach to tone, space, and emotional subtlety as a foundational influence. His work demonstrated that keyboards could be central to a band's sound, not merely supplementary, opening new possibilities for textural experimentation in popular music.

Wright's influence also lay in his philosophy of musical restraint and collaborative balance. By prioritizing the overall sound over individual display, he exemplified a model of musicianship that valued cohesion, atmosphere, and emotional resonance. This approach encouraged other artists to consider the role of each instrument as part of a larger compositional tapestry, contributing to the evolution of modern rock arrangements where texture and mood are as important as melody or rhythm.

Analysis of Key Songs and Albums

An analysis of key songs and albums reveals the depth and versatility of Wright's contributions to Pink Floyd and his broader musical legacy. On The Dark Side of the Moon,

Wright's work on tracks like Us and Them and The Great Gig in the Sky exemplifies his mastery of emotional texture and harmonic layering. In Us and Them, his electric piano and synthesizer pads provide a spacious, reflective backdrop that complements Waters' lyrical commentary and Gilmour's melodic phrasing. In The Great Gig in the Sky, his harmonic support frames the iconic vocal performance, enhancing the song's emotional power without overshadowing it.

Wish You Were Here further demonstrates Wright's influence on conceptually driven music. On Shine On You Crazy Diamond, his Hammond organ, electric piano, and synthesizer layers create the vast, haunting atmosphere that defines the piece. Wright's use of sustained chords, subtle harmonic shifts, and interwoven textures provides continuity across the song's extended sections, allowing the narrative tribute to Syd Barrett to unfold with emotional resonance. In Have a Cigar and Welcome to the Machine, his textural contributions support the critique of the music industry, blending seamlessly with Gilmour's guitar and Mason's percussion to create cohesive sonic statements.

In Animals, Wright's role in Dogs and Sheep highlights his ability to translate thematic concepts into musical textures. His keyboard work reinforces the narrative arcs, creating tension, suspense, and contrast through harmonic choices and layered synth passages. Wright's contributions demonstrate his capacity to support storytelling through music, emphasizing atmosphere and emotional impact over overt technical display.

The Division Bell showcases Wright's later work and the maturity of his style. On High Hopes, his expressive piano lines and synthesizer textures provide the emotional core, supporting the reflective lyrics and melodic guitar phrases. Wright's ability to craft music that is simultaneously intimate and expansive underscores the enduring quality of his musicianship and its adaptability across decades of evolution in rock music.

Comparison with Contemporaries and Innovators of the Time

In comparison with contemporaries, Richard Wright's approach to keyboards was unique in its combination of subtlety, textural innovation, and harmonic sophistication. While many keyboardists of the 1960s and 1970s focused on virtuosic displays, flashy solos, or complex classical-inspired techniques, Wright emphasized atmosphere, mood, and collaborative enhancement. This approach aligned him with progressive and experimental innovators but distinguished him through its emotional depth and restraint.

Wright's contemporaries included musicians such as Rick Wakeman of Yes, Keith Emerson of Emerson, Lake and Palmer, and Tony Banks of Genesis. Unlike Wakeman or Emerson, who often foregrounded keyboards with virtuosic solos and elaborate technical flourishes, Wright's work was integrative, serving the composition rather than dominating it. Compared to Banks, who similarly focused on progressive textures, Wright's use of ambient layering, subtle chord shifts, and real-time synthesizer manipulation provided a more atmospheric and emotionally immersive quality.

In the context of rock music innovation, Wright's contributions to synthesizer use were particularly influential. While electronic experimentation was increasingly common in the 1970s, Wright's integration of analog synthesizers into the fabric of rock compositions was pioneering. His ability to manipulate sound parameters, blend textures, and sustain emotional resonance distinguished him from contemporaries who employed synthesizers primarily as effects or novelties. Wright's work demonstrated that electronic keyboards could serve as primary instruments for atmosphere, narrative, and mood, influencing subsequent artists in progressive rock, ambient, and electronic genres.

Moreover, Wright's emphasis on restraint, collaboration, and emotional resonance set him apart from keyboardists who prioritized technical display. His approach demonstrated that subtlety could achieve profound impact, that atmosphere could convey narrative as powerfully as melody, and that keyboards could function as integral components of composition rather than auxiliary instruments. This philosophy has informed generations of musicians seeking to balance innovation, expression, and cohesion within band contexts.

Richard Wright's musical style and legacy are therefore inseparable from both his technical mastery and his conceptual vision. His keyboards were the backbone of Pink Floyd's sonic identity, shaping harmonic structures, defining atmospheres, and supporting narrative expression. Beyond the band, his influence on rock music lies in his pioneering use of synthesizers, his emphasis on textural innovation, and his demonstration of the power of subtlety, restraint, and emotional depth in musical creation. Through key songs, albums, and innovative techniques, Wright established a model of musicianship that continues to resonate with artists and listeners, affirming his place as one of rock's most important and enduring keyboardists.

CHAPTER 12

Personal Life and Challenges

Richard Wright's personal life was marked by both stability and change, reflecting the complexities of a musician navigating fame, creative pressures, and intimate relationships. In 1964, Wright married his first wife, Juliette Gale, who had been a singer in one of the early bands that eventually evolved into Pink Floyd. Their shared musical interests created a strong initial bond, as both were committed to creative pursuits and the emerging London music scene. Together, they had two children, and Wright balanced the responsibilities of fatherhood with the demands of an evolving musical career. This period of his life was one of both personal and professional growth, as he honed his skills in Pink Floyd while nurturing a family life that required emotional investment and stability.

The marriage with Juliette Gale lasted until 1982, ending after nearly two decades. During this time, Wright faced the challenges of maintaining personal relationships while contributing to a band that was becoming internationally renowned. The pressures of touring, recording, and the interpersonal dynamics within Pink Floyd often left little time for private life, creating strains that contributed to the eventual dissolution of his first marriage. Despite the end of the marriage, Wright maintained a close relationship with his children, striving to remain present in their lives and to provide guidance and support while balancing his demanding professional commitments.

In 1984, Wright entered a second marriage with Franka. This period marked a renewed chapter in his personal life, allowing him to seek stability and companionship outside the intense creative environment of Pink Floyd. The marriage lasted a decade, ending in 1994. While details of this relationship remain private, it is clear that it provided Wright with a source of personal grounding during a period of professional transition. The balance between personal commitments and professional obligations continued to be a theme in Wright's life, influencing both his emotional well-being and his approach to creativity.

In 1995, Wright married his third wife, Mildred Hobbs, known as Millie. This relationship coincided with some of Wright's most introspective musical work, including his 1996 solo album Broken China, which explored themes of mental health, personal struggle, and emotional complexity. Millie's experiences with depression became a central inspiration for the album, reflecting Wright's empathy and his willingness to channel personal experiences into creative expression. Their marriage also brought the birth of their son, Ben, adding a new dimension of fatherhood later in Wright's life. The relationship with Millie represented both emotional intimacy and creative inspiration, demonstrating the interplay between Wright's personal life and musical output. They eventually separated in 2007, but their time together left a lasting impact on Wright's personal and artistic development.

Wright's family connections extended beyond his immediate household. His daughter Gala married Guy Pratt, a bassist who collaborated extensively with Pink Floyd after the departure of Roger Waters. This connection not only reinforced Wright's family ties but also linked his personal and professional worlds, as his children became part of the broader network of musicians associated with the band. These relationships underscore the interconnectedness of Wright's personal life with his musical career, revealing the way family, friendship, and creative collaboration often overlapped in his life.

Health Struggles, Emotional Challenges, and Personal Reflections

Wright's personal life was shaped by a series of health challenges and emotional experiences that influenced both his daily life and his artistic work. While he maintained a relatively private demeanor, close friends and family observed the pressures and anxieties that arose from a career in a high-profile rock band. The rigors of touring, the demands of recording, and the stress of interpersonal conflicts within Pink Floyd often affected his emotional and mental health. Wright's quiet and introspective nature meant that he processed these challenges internally, finding expression in music rather than public discourse.

The experiences within his marriages and family life also contributed to periods of emotional struggle. The end of his first and second marriages coincided with periods of personal reflection, as he navigated feelings of loss, change, and adaptation. These experiences were not isolated from his musical work; rather, they informed the emotive quality of his compositions. Wright's sensitivity to emotional nuance allowed him to translate personal experiences into musical atmospheres, chordal textures, and melodic motifs. His work on Broken China is a vivid example, exploring themes of mental health and human vulnerability in a way that was both empathetic and musically sophisticated. The album's focus on Millie's battle with depression demonstrates how personal challenges became catalysts for artistic exploration, reflecting Wright's capacity for deep empathy and emotional engagement.

Throughout his life, Wright confronted the pressures of public expectation, professional responsibility, and personal vulnerability. Despite these challenges, he maintained a remarkable resilience, continuing to contribute to Pink Floyd's albums, tours, and creative processes even when facing significant personal obstacles. His reflective and contemplative nature allowed him to balance emotional difficulties with creative output, channeling personal challenges into music that resonated with both intimate and universal themes.

How Personal Experiences Influenced His Music

Richard Wright's personal experiences were inextricably linked to his musical output. His introspective personality, combined with periods of personal struggle and familial responsibility, informed the contemplative, atmospheric, and emotionally resonant qualities of his compositions. The tensions, losses, and joys of his personal life provided rich material for musical expression, allowing him to create works that reflected the depth and complexity of human experience.

For example, Wright's early family life, including his role as a husband and father, influenced his sensitivity to melody, harmony, and texture. The need for balance, care, and attentiveness in family relationships mirrored his approach to music, where each note and chord was placed with deliberate intention to support the overall emotional effect. His experience of love, loss, and reconciliation informed the emotional shading in his playing, from the haunting ethereal textures on Wish You Were Here to the reflective keyboard layers on The Division Bell.

Wright's personal struggles with health, emotional well-being, and the challenges of fame also shaped his music. Albums like Broken China explicitly drew from his experiences, translating empathy, concern, and emotional depth into musical forms. Even in Pink Floyd's collective work, his personal insights influenced the harmonic and textural decisions that defined the band's sound. Wright's quiet presence allowed him to observe and internalize emotional and social dynamics, later transforming these observations into evocative music that communicated subtle psychological and emotional landscapes.

The influence of his relationships on his music was particularly evident in the interplay between harmony and mood. Wright often used minor chordal shifts, ambient textures, and sustained harmonics to convey melancholy, introspection, or empathy. Conversely, his use of major harmonies, brighter textures, and lyrical melodies reflected moments of personal contentment, hope, or connection. This nuanced translation of life experience into musical expression contributed to the enduring emotional resonance of his work and solidified his role as a foundational architect of Pink Floyd's sound.

Stories That Reveal His Character and Resilience

Stories from Wright's life reveal a man of subtle strength, resilience, and integrity. Despite the pressures of fame and the personal challenges he faced, Wright maintained a composed and reflective demeanor. Colleagues often described him as patient, diplomatic, and thoughtful, willing to support others' creative visions while asserting his own in measured, effective ways. His ability to navigate professional conflicts, such as the tensions surrounding The Wall, while maintaining personal and artistic dignity demonstrates remarkable resilience.

Wright's response to personal challenges, including marital changes, health issues, and family responsibilities, further illustrates his character. He balanced professional obligations with private life, ensuring that his children, spouses, and close friends remained a priority even amid the demands of international touring and high-stakes recording projects. His empathy, cultivated through these experiences, informed his musical output, resulting in compositions that conveyed understanding, compassion, and emotional subtlety.

The creation of Broken China offers perhaps the clearest insight into Wright's character. By transforming Millie's struggles with depression into a nuanced musical narrative, he demonstrated empathy, creative sensitivity, and emotional courage. He did not shy away from difficult emotional material but instead used it to craft art that could communicate, comfort, and resonate with listeners. This approach reflects both personal resilience and an understanding of music as a vehicle for human connection and emotional exploration.

Through the combination of family experiences, personal challenges, and creative responses, Wright's life reveals a

110

musician who integrated private reflection, emotional intelligence, and artistic sensitivity into every aspect of his work. His character, marked by resilience, patience, and subtle strength, was inseparable from his musical legacy, influencing both the sound of Pink Floyd and the emotional depth of his solo projects. Wright's personal life and challenges not only shaped his art but also revealed the enduring human qualities that allowed him to navigate fame, creativity, and adversity with grace and insight.

CHAPTER 13

Later Years and Last Contributions

Following the monumental success of The Division Bell and the associated tours in the mid-1990s, Richard Wright entered a period characterized by reflection, selective musical engagement, and careful consideration of his artistic contributions. Though he had been a central figure in Pink Floyd's earlier decades, Wright's later years were defined by a more measured pace of activity, balancing his desire to create music with the need for personal equilibrium.

During this period, Wright remained connected to Pink Floyd through various projects, including retrospective releases, remastering of classic albums, and occasional involvement in archival or commemorative projects. While he was not pursuing a full-scale touring schedule or solo album production at the same intensity as earlier decades, he contributed thoughtfully to maintaining the band's legacy and ensuring that their recorded works retained their original sonic integrity. His work involved revisiting recordings, consulting on remastering projects, and collaborating with engineers to enhance sound quality while preserving the atmosphere and textures that defined Pink Floyd's music.

Wright also explored smaller-scale musical projects that allowed him to experiment freely without the constraints of large-scale production or commercial expectations. These efforts included composing and recording new material, sometimes for personal satisfaction, and occasionally for release in limited formats or charitable projects. His continued focus on keyboards, synthesizers, and harmonic experimentation reflected his enduring curiosity and technical expertise. Even in the quieter phases of his career, Wright's approach to music remained deeply considered, emphasizing tonal richness, atmospheric layering, and emotional resonance.

Throughout this time, Wright's work reflected a mature understanding of his artistic identity. No longer seeking to prove himself or dominate the creative process, he concentrated on refining the qualities that had always defined his style: subtlety, textural depth, and the creation of immersive soundscapes. This period demonstrated that his influence extended beyond performance or composition; his judgment, taste, and conceptual sensibility contributed to the careful curation of Pink Floyd's legacy and the preservation of the band's musical ethos.

Collaborations, Interviews, and Public Appearances

Even as he focused on selective musical projects, Richard Wright engaged in collaborations, interviews, and public appearances that reinforced his enduring influence and deepened public understanding of his role in Pink Floyd. Collaborations during these years were often understated but significant, allowing him to contribute his distinctive keyboard work and harmonic insights to projects outside the immediate framework of Pink Floyd. These collaborations included guest performances, studio sessions for other artists, and participation in soundtracks or multimedia projects where his expertise in atmospheric and textural composition could be effectively applied.

Wright also participated in interviews, documentaries, and retrospectives that explored the history, creative process, and cultural impact of Pink Floyd. His reflections offered insight into both the collaborative dynamics of the band and his personal philosophy as a musician. Wright spoke candidly about the challenges of balancing individual creativity with collective goals, the importance of subtlety and restraint in musical expression, and the evolving nature of the band's sound across decades. These interviews contributed to a more nuanced public understanding of his role, highlighting his contributions not merely as a keyboardist but as a conceptual and emotional anchor within the group.

Public appearances during this period were carefully managed and selective. Wright often attended events honoring Pink Floyd's achievements, such as awards ceremonies, tributes, and fan gatherings. His presence reinforced the continuity of the band's legacy while allowing him to maintain personal privacy and focus on his artistic priorities. These appearances demonstrated his commitment to honoring the collective achievements of Pink Floyd while preserving the dignity and subtlety that had defined his personal and professional demeanor throughout his career.

Additionally, Wright's participation in collaborative projects and public discourse provided opportunities to mentor and inspire younger musicians. He shared insights into keyboard technique, compositional approach, and atmospheric layering, emphasizing the importance of creativity, intuition, and attention to tonal detail. Through these engagements, he reinforced his influence not only as a performer but also as a guiding voice for subsequent generations of artists navigating the complex interplay of technical skill, musical sensibility, and emotional expression.

Final Recordings and Projects

Richard Wright's final recordings and projects reflected both a culmination of his lifelong artistic principles and a continued desire to explore new musical possibilities. He maintained a meticulous approach to studio work, carefully constructing textures, harmonies, and melodic lines that aligned with his signature style while accommodating contemporary production techniques. His contributions were often characterized by clarity, depth, and an emotional resonance that distinguished his playing from more conventional keyboard approaches.

One of the notable aspects of Wright's final projects was his continued emphasis on collaboration, even in a reduced or advisory capacity. He often worked closely with engineers, producers, and fellow musicians to ensure that recordings retained the integrity, atmosphere, and subtlety characteristic of his work. These sessions highlighted his adaptability, technical mastery, and unwavering commitment to musical quality, illustrating that his contributions were equally valuable in the studio and in conceptual planning.

Wright's last projects also included participation in commemorative works, live recordings, and archival releases that celebrated Pink Floyd's history. His involvement ensured that the band's legacy was presented authentically and with attention to detail, reflecting his enduring concern for musical and historical accuracy. These projects often required revisiting material from earlier decades, integrating new technological possibilities, and providing insights into arrangement, harmonization, and textural design. Wright's contributions reinforced the importance of continuity and integrity in the curation of musical history.

In addition to studio work, Wright occasionally composed and recorded material intended for more personal projects or limited release. These compositions often emphasized introspection, subtle melodic development, and atmospheric layering, reflecting his lifelong approach to music as an expressive, immersive medium. Even in these final creative efforts, Wright maintained his commitment to emotional resonance, harmonic sophistication, and textural depth, demonstrating the consistency and maturity of his artistic vision.

Legacy-Building Actions Before His Passing

In the later years of his life, Richard Wright was deeply invested in consolidating his legacy, both as an individual musician and as a foundational member of Pink Floyd. This involved ensuring that his contributions were properly recognized, preserving the integrity of recordings and performances, and mentoring younger musicians and collaborators who could continue to advance the principles he had championed.

Wright took deliberate steps to ensure that his work within Pink Floyd was accurately represented and celebrated. He participated in remastering projects, archival releases, and commemorative editions of classic albums, offering guidance on sound quality, tonal balance, and textual accuracy. These actions preserved the subtle nuances of his keyboard work and ensured that future listeners would experience the music as he had intended, with its emotional and harmonic intricacies intact.

In addition to technical legacy-building, Wright also engaged in reflective and educational activities. Through interviews, public discussions, and selective teaching engagements, he shared insights into his compositional philosophy, approach to keyboards and synthesizers, and the emotional and collaborative principles that had guided his career. These actions reinforced his role as a mentor and cultural contributor, ensuring that his approach to music could inform and inspire future generations of musicians and audiences.

Wright's commitment to legacy extended to live performance and public celebration. Even as his health and personal priorities limited extensive touring, he participated in final appearances that honored Pink Floyd's history and influence. These performances highlighted his enduring musical presence, allowing audiences to experience his contributions firsthand and ensuring that the emotional and textural qualities of his playing remained a living aspect of the band's legacy.

Finally, Wright's personal philosophy of restraint, collaboration, and emotional expression influenced the way he approached the final chapters of his life. Rather than seeking personal acclaim, he focused on sustaining the integrity of his work, enriching collective projects, and sharing his musical wisdom. This approach reinforced the enduring value of his contributions and ensured that his legacy would be measured not merely by technical skill, but by the depth, subtlety, and emotional resonance that defined his career.

Through careful stewardship of recordings, thoughtful participation in projects, and dedication to mentorship, Richard Wright ensured that his influence would endure beyond his lifetime. His final years reflected a synthesis of technical mastery, artistic integrity, and emotional insight, consolidating a legacy that spans decades of innovation, creativity, and subtle yet profound impact on rock music and keyboard performance.

CHAPTER 14

Death and Posthumous Recognition

Richard Wright passed away on September 15, 2008, at the age of sixty-five, after a courageous battle with cancer. His illness, which had been privately managed in its early stages, became publicly known as fans and media outlets expressed concern for his well-being during his final months. Despite the physical and emotional challenges posed by his condition, Wright continued to maintain a dignified and introspective presence, reflecting the composed and reserved persona that had defined both his public image and his approach to music throughout his career.

The timing of Wright's death resonated deeply within the context of Pink Floyd's history. He passed less than three years after the passing of Syd Barrett, another foundational member whose creativity had left a profound mark on the band's early sound. Wright's death marked the loss of a musician who had been central to the development of Pink Floyd's unique atmosphere and emotional depth, and it symbolized the closing of an important period in rock music's history.

Wright's final months were characterized by reflection, close connections with family, and continued engagement with music in ways that were physically and emotionally feasible. Although he was no longer touring extensively or engaged in full-scale recording projects, he remained attentive to the preservation of his artistic legacy. Friends and collaborators noted that Wright approached his illness with quiet dignity, focusing on the meaningful aspects of life and work rather than dwelling on the challenges of his condition.

His passing was sudden in its finality, yet it was also the culmination of a life marked by careful attention to artistic integrity, personal reflection, and a commitment to collaborative creativity. The circumstances of his death underscored the fragility of life but also highlighted the enduring value of the contributions he had made over decades of musical exploration, innovation, and performance.

Reactions from Fans, Peers, and the Music Industry

The reaction to Richard Wright's death was immediate, heartfelt, and far-reaching, reflecting the profound impact he had on fans, peers, and the music industry. Fans around the world expressed deep sorrow at the loss of a musician whose work had defined the soundtracks of countless lives. Messages of tribute and remembrance appeared across media platforms, emphasizing not only his technical skill but also the emotional resonance and subtle artistry that characterized his music. Many fans highlighted the sense of atmosphere, reflection, and emotional depth that Wright's keyboards brought to Pink Floyd's compositions, noting that his contributions had often been understated yet central to the band's enduring appeal.

Peers and fellow musicians also reacted with admiration and profound respect. Members of Pink Floyd, including David Gilmour and Nick Mason, released statements expressing grief at the loss of a friend and collaborator. Gilmour described Wright as a musician whose touch and sensibility had been fundamental to the identity of the band, emphasizing the elegance, subtlety, and emotional insight that he brought to every recording and performance. Mason reflected on Wright's quiet yet powerful presence, noting that his musicianship had often served as the harmonic and emotional glue that bound the band's work together.

The broader music industry recognized Wright's death as the passing of an innovator who had transformed the role of keyboards in rock music. Critics, journalists, and historians highlighted his pioneering use of synthesizers, textural layering, and harmonic sophistication, emphasizing that his approach had expanded the possibilities of keyboard performance within popular music. Tributes acknowledged that Wright's influence extended beyond Pink Floyd, shaping ambient, progressive, and electronic music in ways that continue to resonate with contemporary artists.

International reactions further demonstrated the global reach of Wright's impact. Media outlets in Europe, North America, and beyond featured retrospectives on his life, career, and contributions to Pink Floyd. Fans held informal gatherings, online memorials, and listening events in his honor, demonstrating the extent to which his work had touched multiple generations. Musicians and industry figures shared personal anecdotes of collaboration, mentorship, and inspiration, reinforcing the sense that Wright's presence had been both artistically transformative and personally significant to those who had worked with him.

Awards, Tributes, and Memorial Events

Following Richard Wright's death, a series of awards, tributes, and memorial events celebrated his life and contributions. Formal recognition came from music institutions and industry bodies, which highlighted his pioneering work on keyboards, his integral role in Pink Floyd's success, and his broader influence on rock music. Posthumous honors included inductions into halls of fame, commemorative awards for lifetime achievement, and recognition of his influence on both peers and emerging artists. These accolades served to formally acknowledge the importance of Wright's contributions to the development of rock music, particularly in terms of harmonic sophistication, atmospheric innovation, and textural creativity.

Memorial events further honored Wright's legacy. Tribute concerts and gatherings featured performances of key Pink Floyd material, highlighting the distinctive keyboard textures and atmospheric contributions that Wright had crafted over decades. These events allowed musicians and fans alike to experience firsthand the emotional power and technical brilliance of his work, reinforcing the enduring relevance of his music. Special editions of Pink Floyd albums, remastered recordings, and commemorative releases also celebrated his artistic achievements, providing historical context and emphasizing the integral role of his musicianship in the band's signature sound.

Additionally, personal tributes from fellow band members and collaborators highlighted Wright's character and professional ethos. Gilmour and Mason spoke at memorials and in interviews about his intelligence, humility, and creative insight. They emphasized the collaborative spirit he embodied, his ability to enhance the work of others without overshadowing them, and the elegance and subtlety of his musical approach. These reflections contributed to a more nuanced public understanding of Wright's influence and reinforced the notion that his legacy was inseparable from both his artistry and his character.

Fans also organized informal tributes, including listening sessions, online commemorations, and gatherings to share memories and reflections. These activities demonstrated that Wright's impact extended beyond formal recognition, resonating deeply with those who had been moved by his music, inspired by his technique, or personally touched by his presence in recordings and performances. The combination of institutional honors and grassroots memorials created a multi-faceted recognition of his contributions, cementing his place in the cultural and musical landscape.

The Enduring Impact of His Life and Music

Richard Wright's enduring impact is evident in the continued influence of his musical style, the ongoing relevance of Pink Floyd's recordings, and the recognition of his contributions to modern rock and keyboard performance. His approach to keyboards, emphasizing atmosphere, texture, and emotional resonance, has informed generations of musicians, inspiring artists across progressive rock, ambient, electronic, and contemporary music genres. Wright's subtle yet sophisticated techniques demonstrated that keyboards could be central to compositional identity, shaping mood, narrative, and harmonic structure in ways previously underexplored in rock music.

His legacy also extends to the philosophy of collaboration and musical restraint. Wright exemplified how musicians could contribute profoundly to a collective sound while maintaining humility, sensitivity, and emotional intelligence. His ability to balance technical proficiency with aesthetic judgment and collaborative harmony continues to serve as a model for contemporary artists navigating the interplay between individual expression and group dynamics.

In addition, Wright's life and work have left an indelible mark on the broader cultural perception of Pink Floyd. His textural contributions and atmospheric layering are recognized as essential elements in the band's signature sound, from the early psychedelic explorations to the complex conceptual projects of later decades. The emotional resonance, subtlety, and spatial sophistication that characterized his playing have become benchmarks against which subsequent keyboardists and producers measure their work.

Posthumous analyses of Wright's contributions highlight the depth, intelligence, and emotional complexity of his musicianship. Critics, scholars, and historians continue to examine his influence on both recorded music and live performance, noting that his understated approach allowed Pink Floyd to achieve its cinematic and immersive qualities. The continuing popularity of Pink Floyd's albums, their ongoing influence on emerging artists, and the persistent appreciation of Wright's keyboard work underscore the lasting nature of his legacy.

Finally, the combination of professional achievements, artistic integrity, and personal humility has ensured that Richard Wright's legacy is multidimensional. He is remembered not only for his technical innovations and compositional skills but also for his character, collaborative spirit, and ability to elevate the music of those around him. His passing marked the conclusion of an extraordinary career, yet his influence persists in the music of countless artists, the continued enjoyment of Pink Floyd's recordings, and the appreciation of audiences worldwide. Wright's life and music remain a testament to the enduring power of subtlety, intelligence, and emotional depth in creating art that resonates across generations.

CHAPTER 15

Legacy and Influence

Richard Wright's influence on modern rock is profound and enduring, primarily because of his pioneering approach to keyboards, harmonic structure, and textural layering. Unlike many of his contemporaries who emphasized technical virtuosity or showmanship, Wright focused on the emotional and atmospheric potential of his instruments. This philosophy reshaped the role of keyboards in rock music, positioning them as central components capable of shaping mood, supporting complex arrangements, and elevating the overall sonic experience.

Wright's approach to synthesizers was particularly innovative for the time. He embraced analog synthesizers and early electronic instruments, such as the EMS VCS 3 and ARP String Ensemble, integrating them into Pink Floyd's compositions with finesse. He utilized these tools not as gimmicks but as integral components of song structure, creating textures that were both forward-looking and emotionally resonant. Tracks such as Shine On You Crazy Diamond, On the Run, and Us and Them showcase Wright's ability to construct immersive soundscapes that guide the listener's experience, demonstrating that keyboards could function as more than accompaniment and could drive narrative, mood, and conceptual depth.

His harmonic sensibility also left a lasting mark on rock music. Wright's sophisticated chord voicings, modal choices, and layered textures influenced not only keyboardists but also composers and arrangers working across genres. By balancing simplicity with subtle complexity, he demonstrated that keyboards could evoke profound emotional response without overwhelming the song's core structure. This approach encouraged a generation of rock musicians to explore texture, atmosphere, and emotional nuance rather than relying solely on speed, technical complexity, or flash.

Moreover, Wright's techniques continue to influence modern keyboardists, especially those in progressive rock, ambient, and experimental genres. Musicians today often cite his use of sustained chords, contrapuntal lines, and the strategic integration of synthesizers with traditional keyboards as inspiration. The emphasis on spatial awareness, layering, and dynamic contrast has become a standard in contemporary rock and electronic music, illustrating how Wright's innovations transcended his era to shape the way keyboards are conceptualized and utilized.

Inspiration to Future Generations of Musicians

Beyond technical influence, Wright inspired future generations of musicians through his philosophy of musical restraint, collaboration, and emotive playing. He demonstrated that artistic impact does not require dominance, aggression, or constant technical display. Instead, he showed that subtlety, listening, and responsiveness within a group setting can be just as powerful. For young musicians studying Pink Floyd's recordings, Wright represents a model of creativity that emphasizes collaboration, balance, and emotional depth.

Many contemporary artists have explicitly acknowledged Wright's inspiration in interviews and discussions. Keyboardists, composers, and producers frequently reference his work when discussing the creation of atmospheric textures or the construction of immersive musical worlds. His influence extends beyond rock into ambient, electronic, and cinematic music, as his techniques in layering and textural development are applicable across a wide spectrum of genres. Wright's music continues to serve as a blueprint for artists seeking to combine technical skill with emotional and conceptual depth, illustrating the enduring relevance of his approach.

Wright's influence also extends to compositional philosophy. He emphasized that music is not only a collection of notes but a means of storytelling, emotional exploration, and conceptual expression. This principle has inspired musicians to consider the narrative and spatial dimensions of their work, encouraging them to create pieces that are holistic, immersive, and emotionally resonant. Wright's legacy in this regard is perhaps as significant as his technical innovations, shaping the mindset of musicians who prioritize musicality, cohesion, and expressiveness in their work.

The Lasting Importance of His Work with Pink Floyd

Richard Wright's work with Pink Floyd remains a cornerstone of his legacy, exemplifying his artistic vision, technical mastery, and collaborative genius. Throughout the band's discography, Wright's keyboards provided the harmonic foundation, emotional depth, and atmospheric cohesion that allowed Pink Floyd's music to transcend conventional rock structures. Albums such as The Dark Side of the Moon, Wish You Were Here, Animals, and The Division Bell demonstrate the enduring significance of his contributions, from melodic support to complex textural layering.

Wright's influence within Pink Floyd is evident in the band's signature sound. His ability to blend piano, organ, and synthesizers seamlessly with guitars, bass, drums, and vocals created a sonic environment that was rich, expansive, and immersive. This approach allowed the band to explore long-form compositions, conceptual albums, and intricate arrangements while maintaining emotional clarity and cohesion. The enduring popularity of these works underscores the importance of Wright's musicianship, as his contributions remain central to the identity and appeal of Pink Floyd decades after their release.

In addition, Wright's work with Pink Floyd has had a lasting impact on the broader music industry. His techniques have informed the approaches of countless bands and artists seeking to create atmosphere, mood, and narrative depth in their music. His integration of electronic and traditional keyboards, his mastery of space and dynamics, and his attention to emotional nuance have set a standard for musical excellence and innovation that continues to inspire musicians worldwide.

Wright's collaborative philosophy also reinforced the lasting value of his work. By prioritizing the collective sound over individual recognition, he contributed to the creation of music that is greater than the sum of its parts. This approach not only shaped Pink Floyd's enduring success but also served as a model for other artists navigating the balance between personal expression and group dynamics. His legacy within the band exemplifies how artistic humility, sensitivity, and dedication to the musical vision can yield work of timeless significance.

Reflections on His Life, Career, and Enduring Presence in Music History

Reflecting on Richard Wright's life and career reveals a musician whose contributions were both profound and understated. While not always in the spotlight, his influence permeated every aspect of Pink Floyd's work and extended into the broader musical landscape. Wright's career exemplifies the power of subtlety, restraint, and emotional intelligence in creating art that resonates across time.

Wright's life story also serves as a testament to resilience, creativity, and adaptability. From his early days experimenting with keyboards and exploring musical textures, to his pivotal role in Pink Floyd's rise, to his later years of selective engagement and legacy preservation, Wright consistently demonstrated artistic integrity and thoughtful musicianship. His career reflects an understanding that influence is not measured solely by visibility or acclaim, but by the enduring impact of one's work on others and the ongoing resonance of musical contributions.

His enduring presence in music history is reinforced by the continued study, performance, and appreciation of Pink Floyd's catalog. Wright's keyboard work is celebrated for its sophistication, emotional resonance, and textural richness, and it remains a reference point for students, musicians, and critics examining the evolution of modern rock. His ability to create immersive atmospheres and convey complex emotional narratives through keyboards alone is widely regarded as a benchmark of excellence and innovation.

Ultimately, Richard Wright's legacy is multi-dimensional. It encompasses technical mastery, compositional innovation, emotional depth, collaborative skill, and the cultivation of enduring influence on future generations. His work reminds us that musicianship can be profound without being ostentatious, that subtlety can convey extraordinary emotional power, and that contributions to collective artistry are as vital as individual virtuosity. Wright's life and music continue to inspire admiration, study, and emulation, ensuring that his influence on rock music and keyboard performance remains vital, enduring, and universally acknowledged.

His story reinforces the notion that true artistic legacy is measured not only by immediate success or recognition but by the lasting resonance of one's work, the inspiration provided to others, and the timeless quality of creative contributions. In this regard, Richard Wright stands among the most influential and respected figures in modern music history, leaving a footprint that will continue to shape musicians, compositions, and the understanding of what keyboards can achieve in the context of rock, ambient, and progressive music.

Printed in Dunstable, United Kingdom